# TARZAN OF THE MOVIES

# TARZAN OF THE MOVIES

**A PICTORIAL HISTORY OF MORE THAN FIFTY YEARS OF EDGAR RICE BURROUGHS' LEGENDARY HERO**

by GABE ESSOE

CADILLAC PUBLISHING CO., INC.
220 Fifth Avenue, New York, N.Y. 10001

This edition published by Cadillac Publishing Co., Inc., by
arrangement with The Citadel Press.

Manufactured in the United States of America
Designed by A. Christopher Simon
Library of Congress catalog card number: 68-28454

*To my beloved Donna*

# TABLE OF CONTENTS

## ACKNOWLEDGEMENTS:

# THE HELPING HANDS

The following is a wonderful group of people, without the help and cooperation of any one of which the book in its present form would hardly have been possible.

Forry Ackerman
Paul Allen
Bruce Bennett
Mike Berman
Dale Broadhurst
Doug Brooks
Hully Burroughs
Camile Cazedessus, Jr.
Virginia Chalmers
Earl Colgrove
Vern Coriell
Ken Dixon
Braven Dyer, Jr.
Chuck Essoe
Gabriella Essoe
Robert Fenton
Mike Henry

Bob Hodes
Ray Lee
Sol Lesser
Roberta Lewis
Frank Merrill
Denny Miller
Jim and Joan
    Burroughs Pierce
Bob Pike
Bill Schroeder
Lillian Schwartz
Loran Smith
Dave Spencer
Van
Stan Vinson
Pat Watson
Gregg Way
Sy Weintraub

Edgar Rice Burroughs, Inc.

TARZANA, CALIFORNIA 91356

1875 - 1950

# FOREWORD

Tarzan of the Apes is an important member of the Burroughs family. In addition to growing up on the Tarzan novels written by my dad, Edgar Rice Burroughs, we have been very close to the Tarzan movies.

I, personally, can vouch for our involvement in films because I married Jim Pierce, the lead in the last silent Tarzan feature picture, *Tarzan and the Golden Lion,* in 1928. He, as Tarzan, and I, as Jane, also made the first radio serialization of dad's books in the early 1930s. This series authentically followed his writings.

My father was never able to understand why the Tarzan motion pictures would not follow his stories more closely. He wrote such a fantastic wealth of material and it seemed to him that some of it should have been suitable for the screen. Instead, Hollywood writers changed the stories and created their own version of dad's hero. For years he tried in vain to get film producers to maintain an integrity with his work. Finally, he gave up, frustrated, and let them do what they were going to do anyway.

It is the hope of ERB, Incorporated, and the entire family that someday we will eventually see films produced from the Tarzan books as they were written. If by no other means possible, we may even produce the films ourselves.

JOAN BURROUGHS PIERCE
*Apple Valley, California • February 29, 1968*

# TARZAN OF THE MOVIES

Edgar Rice Burroughs

The world's first glimpse of Tarzan was on the cover of *All-Story* magazine in October 1912, in an illustration by Clinton Pettee

# INTRODUCTION

Not often does a literary work inspire a series of films. And it is rare indeed that one becomes a continuing screen effort to the point that, in effect, it establishes careers for a large number of actors. But that is exactly what Edgar Rice Burroughs' *Tarzan of the Apes* has achieved.

ERB's fantastic creation has (in all likelihood) directly affected more lives than any other character in fiction. "How much would heredity," ERB mused on a sleepless night in 1911, "influence character if the infant were transplanted to an entirely different environment and raised there?" For his fictional experiment, he put a babe of the English nobility into the jungles to be brought up by apes. ". . . And the boy-child was called Tarzan," which is ape-talk for "white-skin."

It is ironical that in dealing with environments, ERB himself created an environment, the movie role of Tarzan, into which actors are placed to suffer its consequences. There has been no other screen role that has involved as many faces. Nor has any other screen role been as physically de-

manding on its players or so crucial to so many careers.

Little did ERB realize then the potential of his fictional hero. He could not have guessed that Tarzan would become an international figure, idolized by millions. He could not have known that his brain-child would make him wealthier than in his most satisfying dreams. In fact, he thought the story poor and doubted its salability, until *All-Story Magazine* purchased it in 1912 for $700.

That sale was the turning point in Burroughs' life, which up to that time had been a rather extravagant string of ineffectualities.

Born September 1, 1875, in Chicago, ERB was a drifter until he was thirty-six, failing in every enterprise he attempted. As a youth, he was dismissed from Phillips Academy in Massachusetts; he flunked the examination for West Point, and was later discharged from the U.S. Cavalry because of a weak heart. He was a cattle drover in Idaho, an Oregon miner, a railroad cop in Utah, a door-to-door salesman, accountant, and business

1

Tarzan as envisioned by
J. Allen St. John for the
cover of *Tarzan and the
Golden Lion*

consultant. When he applied for a commission with Teddy Roosevelt's Rough Riders, he was turned down.

He was the kind of man who would take on any job to try to get rich quick, but without ever pulling it off. Most of the time he was unable to support his wife and children adequately.

At the time he began to write, his independent mail order business had just flopped and he was a sales agent for pencil sharpeners, with headquarters in borrowed office space.

While drifting through the unsatisfactory real world, he would console himself with a fantasy world in which he was handsome, virile, and capable of success, the idol of whole civilizations, beyond the limits of credulity. And as his daydreaming became increasingly more necessary to him, he began reading pulp fiction and was appalled at the poor quality of the stories. They

were nowhere equal to his own prodigious imagination.

Although he knew nothing of writing, he felt certain he could produce material more entertaining than what he read. His first story, "Dejah Thoris, Princess of Mars," was submitted in two installments to *All-Story Magazine* under the pen name of Normal Bean (derived from normal head or brain). It was accepted, and the four hundred dollars paid him for that manuscript was one of the biggest thrills of his life.

His story appeared February, 1912, retitled "Under the Moon of Mars." His pen name had been changed by the printer, thinking it was misspelled, to Norman Bean. When he complained to the publisher, he was told that on his next story they would use his real name and avoid further complications.

The alteration of his pen name was not the only

thing he objected to. The check given him in payment had "For All Rights" typed across it, and ERB insisted that the only thing he had sold was first magazine rights. "What other rights are there?" came the question. "I don't know," replied the new author, feeling his way, "maybe moving picture rights, or something else." A volume of correspondence followed on the subject, and *All-Story* finally yielded to ERB's persistence, sending him a letter saying that the author retained all rights on his stories other than first serial rights. Had Burroughs' innate genius not guided him at this crucial stage, he would have had nothing to sell to film makers in later years.

On the success of his first story, he contemplated a literary career and began writing a new adventure tale. "Most of the stories I wrote," ERB once confessed, "were the stories I told myself just before I went to sleep." Such a tale was "Tarzan of the Apes," written in longhand on backs of old letters and odd pieces of paper. He relied on what he remembered of H. M. Stanley's *In Darkest Africa* for background material. When his memory faltered, he fell back on invention, and at one time unwittingly placed a tiger in Africa.

Introduced to the world in October, 1912, via *All-Story,* Tarzan was an immediate sensation, convincing ERB that he had found his trade. As previously agreed, his real name appeared as author under "Tarzan of the Apes" with Norman Bean in parentheses. Fellow daydreamers recognized their master in ERB, who immediately followed his stories with sequels, "The God of Mars" and "The Return of Tarzan," both of which sold for $1,000.

That was the beginning. Two years later, A. C. McClurg & Co., prompted by the widely popular newspaper serialization of the Tarzan stories, asked permission to be allowed to publish them in book form. Months before, McClurg, along with eleven other major publishers, had rejected ERB's queries.

By the time of his death in 1950, Edgar Rice Burroughs had written sixty-seven novels, twenty-six of which dealt with Tarzan. His works have been translated into thirty-one languages and have sold in excess of thirty-six million copies.

Although the forty-one non-Tarzan novels, which include the Mars, Venus and Pellucidar series, for each of which the inventive ERB cre-

ated separate languages, enjoyed their share of popularity, they never received the same acclaim the Apeman did. It was upon this single character that ERB founded an industry.

Four years after Tarzan invaded the hardcover market, the first motion picture based on the story was ready for release. *Tarzan of the Apes,* starring Elmo Lincoln in the title role, opened on Broadway, January 27, 1918. It did standup business all around the country and became one of the first movies in silent screen history to gross over a million dollars. A sequel, *Romance of Tarzan,* was released later that year and was equally successful.

To date there have been fourteen actors to sport the loincloth in forty motion pictures, amassing a total gross of nearly 500 million dollars. The fifteenth on the Tarzan family tree, Ron Ely, has brought the Apeman into millions of homes via the television screen, increasing the Apeman's commercial value immensely.

With royalties from the early Tarzan vehicles, ERB moved his family to California in 1919 and for $125,000 purchased the mansion and 540-acre San Fernando Valley estate of Harrison Gray Otis, publisher of the *Los Angeles Times.* He gratefully renamed the acreage "Tarzana Ranch."

The community surrounding his ranch, anxious to be governmentally recognized, came to ERB on July 9, 1928, to ask his permission to call their city Tarzana. Graciously complying, he added his name to the petition for a U.S. Post Office, which was soon granted. Thereafter, subdividing his property into lots, he sold to businesses and developers and aided in setting city boundaries. He assisted at the inauguration of the Tarzana Chamber of Commerce; then, selling his home to the El Caballero Country Club, he moved to Malibu. At about the same time, Tarzan, Texas, also applied for and was granted a post office.

Meanwhile, deciding that book publishers demanded too great a percentage of the gross returns from his books, he organized Edgar Rice Burroughs, Incorporated—in Tarzana, of course. With himself as president, he proceeded to publish and market his own literary wares and also to consolidate his real estate activities. He always serialized his new novels in magazines before committing them to hardcover, to realize maximum payoff.

To market Tarzan further, he formed a radio division of Edgar Rice Burroughs, Inc., in 1931,

Edgar Rice Burroughs and son John Coleman, who illustrated many of his father's books

and produced a series of Tarzan records. His daughter Joan and son-in-law, former Tarzan Jim Pierce, recorded 364 fifteen-minute episodes as the Apeman and his mate for the serialized radio show. Within two years, ERB had sold the "Tarzan radio act" to stations in every state of the Union, to South America and Western Europe. Through Tarzan, ERB introduced the pre-recorded radio show; up to this time all radio programs had been aired live. Tarzan's pioneering success in this field prompted a major trend toward "canned" broadcasts. Two decades later, a second Tarzan radio series featured the voice of Carlton Kardell.

A year after he branched into radio, ERB contracted with United Feature Syndicate to distribute a Tarzan comic strip internationally. The strip was conceived by Joseph H. Neebe and originally drawn by Hal Foster (of Prince Valiant fame). In its peak popularity year, 1942, 141 daily papers were using the daily strip drawn by Rex Mason from material based on the Tarzan novels; 156 Sunday newspapers were running a full-color

On his beloved Tarzana Ranch, 1923

Burroughs with his grandchildren, John Ralston Burroughs, James Michael Pierce, and Danton Burroughs in 1945

Captain Edgar Rice Burroughs, 1918

page of Tarzan, drawn by Foster from original material by a ghost writer under ERB's supervision. An unconfirmed report indicates that ERB's income from comic strip syndication was nearly $5,000 monthly in the mid-thirties.

In 1936, Tarzan was also launched into comic books as newspaper strip reprints in *Tip-Top Comics*. He also appeared in *Comics on Parade* and *Sparkler Comics*. His own comic magazine was first published in 1947 by Dell Publishing Company in two trial issues, with original stories illustrated by Jesse Marsh. The trial issues were so profitable that Dell went into bi-monthly publication of the *Tarzan Comics* until July, 1951, when it went monthly. Currently, the Tarzan novels are being serialized in *Gold Key Comic Books*, illustrated by noted artist Russ Manning, who also does the daily and Sunday newspaper strip.

Whenever, wherever Tarzan was mentioned, ERB received a cut. He had had the foresight, 'way back in 1913, to register "Tarzan" as a trademark which, over the years, he licensed out to several hundred different manufacturers. The

"Tarzan" products have been innumerable: sweat shirts, wrist watches, masks, candy, trading cards, bubble gum, ice cream cups, inflated rubber toys, buttons, bats, bathing suits, garters, records, coffee. In 1943, over three million loaves of Tarzan bread were sold. By paying a dollar, boys and girls could join the "Tarzan Clan of America" in 1939, a club ERB hoped in vain would some day rival the Boy and Girl Scouts. The start of World War II diminished the Clan's chances of survival.

At the height of his business ambition in 1935, ERB participated in a four-way partnership which formed Burroughs-Tarzan Enterprises, Inc., with the intention of filming a new series of Tarzan epics with authentic scenic background. They hoped to reap that share of motion picture grosses rightfully claimed by major studios. An expedition to Guatemala with Olympic shot-putter Herman Brix resulted in one of the few productions of the company. The film, not entirely an immediate financial boon, was released twice under different titles.

ERB also returned to one of his old vocations, that of providing business counsel. One of his 1935 brochures stated: "We have an organization that is prepared to assist in working out merchandising campaigns for sponsors; and, as owners of the Tarzan copyright and a wide range of Tarzan trademarks, we are in a position to make use of the Tarzan name in many lines." Well-known firms, such as the Signal Oil and Gas Co., Reed Tobacco Co., Royal Baking Powder Co., and the venerable H. J. Heinz Co., subscribed to his service.

All this incredible activity seemed to have no outward effect on him. He continued to dictate his stories four hours a day; he rode horseback, played tennis regularly, learned to fly and bought his own plane. He was so enthusiastic about flying that for a brief time he owned considerable stock in a company that manufactured airplane engines, called Apache Motors, after his book *Apache Devil*.

At sixty, he could have passed for forty-five. He was bald, stocky, and nearly always tan, and he had sharp brown eyes with a curiously genial squint. He spoke in short, quick sentences, like a stock broker with one eye always on the tape, and he allocated his time by the second hand of his watch.

With his highly prized Cord automobile, 1933

Having exploited Tarzan as diligently as possible, ERB made certain that his creation would continue beyond his own life span. He set up a Tarzan dynasty, hoping his three children would eventually manage the corporation.

When business activities softened with the advent of World War II, ERB volunteered his services to the Army as war correspondent. In a column written spasmodically for the *Honolulu Advertiser,* he covered the lighter side of war. His final war report appeared in the *Advertiser* two weeks prior to Japan's unconditional surrender.

The momentum of his great empire failed to

As a war correspondent, 1945

pick up after the war; and ERB, too, tired. He contracted Parkinson's Disease and suffered from a heart ailment. On March 19, 1950, Edgar Rice Burroughs died. His death at age seventy-four was attributed to a heart attack and hardening of the arteries.

Even with the nearly annual Tarzan films, the Apeman slumbered and began to lose popular favor after ERB's death. New interest, however, was aroused in late 1961 when a Downey, California, school teacher removed two Tarzan novels from the school library after a parent had complained that the jungle hero and his mate were living together out of wedlock, and raising an illegitimate child besides.

Tarzan buffs and ERB fans rushed to the rescue, exlaiming that Tarzan and Jane had been married in *The Return of Tarzan* in 1915. Their defensive wailing activated a demand for Tarzan novels that bookstores were unable to meet.

Unable to acquire publishing rights, a couple of New York publishers made a superficial investigation at the United States Copyright Office and came to the erroneous conclusion that the copyrights on a large number of ERB's works had lapsed and had not been renewed. Several national magazines, *Life* included, joined in the dangerous perpetuation of the careless mistake.

Overnight, the market staggered under the deluge of six million unauthorized Tarzan books and paperbacks from a slew of publishers. Even a new Tarzan series by another author, Barton Werper, appeared. Werper, incidentally, was the pseudonym of the writing team of Peter and Peggy Scott.

Since all copyrights were in order, Edgar Rice Burroughs, Inc., began legal enforcement of their rights and prosecution of the profiteers and pirate editions. Decisions in favor of Burroughs' heirs were reached in courts from Minnesota to Kenya to Finland. Nearly eighteen months passed before all Tarzan rights were restored to their rightful owners and the myriad unauthorized Tarzans removed from newsstands and book stores.

The Apeman fared well through the crisis. But when Robert M. Hodes, now vice-president and general manager of ERB, Inc., made the rounds of the major publishers in the country, trying to have the twenty-six Tarzan books published as a series, he was turned down everywhere. The freshly accrued rejections somewhat paralleled ERB's original attempts at publication in 1913.

Then in late 1962, Ian Ballantine of Ballantine Books, Inc., decided to give his faith in Tarzan a try. In a heroic gamble, he suspended all other publication and brought out ten Tarzan titles in each of the next two publishing seasons. Although the new paperback series didn't catch on immediately, by the time all twenty-six titles were in print, Tarzan was a best-seller all over again.

And as if to testify to the new vigorous interest in Burroughs, three biographies, *Edgar Rice Burroughs: Master of Adventure* by Richard Lupoff, *The Big Swingers* by Robert Fenton, and *The*

*Wizard of Tarzana* by Vernell Coriell, have been published recently.

It also seems that author Burroughs has finally received literary recognition. Excerpts from *Tarzan of the Apes* are now printed in English textbooks on both high school and collegiate levels; and Ohio University has selected the entire novel for assigned reading. His work is studied as early twentieth-century American fiction, with literary ties that link Tarzan with Rudyard Kipling's Mowgli, Rousseau's Natural Man, and the mythological Remus and Romulus. The Oxford University Press has also included ERB's first published story, "A Princess of Mars," in an anthology alongside of Charles Dickens, Sir Walter Scott, Sir Arthur Conan Doyle, H. G. Wells, Robert Louis Stevenson, and Jules Verne.

In reality, however, ERB has no literary kinship except in his thematic development. Although some aspects of his style bear a close similarity to Kipling, Stevenson, and Verne, his work is equally similar to the writing in early pulp magazines. On many occasions he admitted that he was no writer. "I write," he confessed once, "to escape . . . to escape poverty."

Because of his lack of a higher education, ERB was guilty of being too verbose, too melodramatic, relying too heavily on coincidences to further his plots, too prone to use flowery language and superfluous adjectives. The element that elevates ERB's work above uninspired potboilers is the tale-telling ability with which he wrote. His stories are packed with action, drama, and suspense, and are never dull reading.

ERB left behind him a literary legacy and the screen legend of Tarzan of the Movies, who has endured two world wars, a depression, several recessions, riots, and love-ins, and will probably continue forever. His company, Edgar Rice Burroughs, Incorporated, flourishes today, a monument to his commercial acumen.

"In an effort to insure that ERB's memory remain intact," explained the young, dynamic Hodes, "we're planning to construct a Burroughs museum. It will house the original manuscripts, first editions of his work, photographs, mementos and all the memorabilia, by-products, and books that we've collected through the years. There will be rooms dedicated to the different worlds ERB created: Venus, Tarzan's jungle, Mars, Pellucidar. We have pledges from the principal Burroughs collectors in the country to donate their entire collections to this project. Adjacent to the Tarzan Room, we intend to have a theatre where all the Tarzan movies ever made will be showing on a continuously scheduled basis.

"In 1965," continued Hodes, "the Tarzana Business and Professional Women's Club made an initial stir about getting behind a monument of this nature, but lack of financial support suspended their activities.

"We intend to be a bit more certain of our plans before we make any formal announcements.

As far as I can see, a museum like this cannot be undertaken until a means of maintenance has been arranged. And since good land is so scarce in this area, we will most likely construct it on the lot behind our office. What we are most sure of is that it will be near a decade before our plans are fully realized."

In any event, upon completion, the museum will stand as a permanent tribute to an energetic and imaginative jack-of-all-trades who attained in life a bigger success than in his wildest daydreams.

Jim Pierce and Joan Burroughs Pierce before a Tarzan-endorsed product, Signal Oil Company, 1933

BOOK ONE
# THE SILENTS

# 1 THE APEMAN'S STRUGGLE TO THE SCREEN

That *Tarzan of the Apes* might be suitable for moving pictures was first suggested to ERB in the winter of 1913 by a New York play broker. Always eager for new enterprises, ERB acquired an agent to crack the potential film market.

Movie producers read the story with interest but felt it was too ambitious for a film venture. The rejections piled up and ERB would have turned his back on the whole idea if he hadn't sold a new manuscript, *The Lad and the Lion*, to Selig Pictures for $500.

Several years later, on June 6, 1916, ERB signed a personal contract with Bill Parsons, a Chicago life insurance salesman, granting him the movie rights to *Tarzan of the Apes*. Parsons was to found a film corporation and sell stock to raise money to produce the picture. The contract stated that ERB was to receive a $5,000 advance on royalties as well as $50,000 worth of capital stock.

Nearly five months later, Parsons paid the author his due and made him the titular Director General of the newly formed National Film Corporation of America.

When *The Lad and the Lion* was released in 1917, ERB was displeased, and complained that it was not his story by the time it reached the screen. He was determined that the same would not happen to his jungle hero. If the Tarzan film were unsuccessful, his writing career would suffer.

Parsons decided on filming *Tarzan of the Apes* near Morgan City, Louisiana, to match some acquired background footage that was shot in Brazil. Ten-year-old Gordon Griffith was chosen to play Tarzan as a boy; and Winslow Wilson, a stocky New York actor and ukelele player, was signed for the lead. Even before actual filming began, the money ran out, and Parsons had to depart to sell more stock.

A few days after production started, World War I broke out and Winslow Wilson, in a patriotic whim, walked off the set to join the Army, leaving the company in the lurch. A frantic search for a substitute began.

Several weeks later, a replacement arrived from Los Angeles. He was Elmo Lincoln, a five-foot 11-1/2 inch, 200-pound athletic character actor, who had once been a peace officer in Arkansas. Lincoln, whose real name was Otto Elmo Linkenhelt, had gotten his first break six years earlier in movie pioneer David Wark Griffith's *The Battle of Elderbush Gulch*. In a stirring fight scene, his shirt was partially torn off, displaying his powerful chest. The great Griffith spied the aforementioned treasure chest and, after the take, motioned Lincoln over to ask his name. When Lincoln told him, Griffith reacted: "Well, young fellow, we'll have to do something about that name if you're going to be in pictures. And I think you should. That's quite a chest you have there."

Under the baptismal guidance of D. W. Griffith, Otto Linkenhelt became Elmo Lincoln. Always featuring Lincoln's massive physique, Griffith cast him in *Birth of a Nation* as a blacksmith; *The Greatest Thing in Life* as a soldier; in *Brute Force*; in *The Kaiser*; and in the Babylonian sequences of *Intolerance* as Belshazzar's bodyguard, "The Mighty Man of Valor."

The twenty-eight-year-old Lincoln left the Griffith lot for the first time to do *Tarzan,* and his barrel-chest made him more suitable for the part than the man he replaced. But because of his gigantic frame, Elmo's tree-perching was kept to a minimum, although for such an enormous man, he was surprisingly agile. He put on a tremendous fight sequence with a lecherous native who tried to carry off his leading lady, Enid Markey, who, in her shy portrayal of Jane Porter, contrasted greatly with Lincoln's vitality.

The fact that Lincoln was not a professional actor didn't matter much for the role. His occasional awkwardness, particularly in the romantic scenes, was happily and surprisingly apt. But since he had little hair of his own, he wore a wig which, although fairly realistic, hampered production when it shifted in the course of heavy action.

In those early days, real apes and monkeys, rightly considered too dangerous, weren't used for films. Consequently, a group of husky young men from the New Orleans Athletic Club were hired to put on ape skins and swing through the trees.

During filming, ERB was on hand to make sure that his novel wasn't distorted. Many fights with Parsons ensued over changes from his story, with Parsons always winning. The scenario, adapted from the book by Fred Miller and Lois Weber, was constantly being altered to facilitate shooting. Near the end, to ERB's horror, they shot with no written script, improvising as they went along.

Even with production liberties, the film remained remarkably faithful to the first book. Lord and Lady Greystoke (True Boardman and Kathleen Kirkham) were marooned on the African coast by a mutinous crew. After giving birth to a child, Lady Greystoke died. Her husband was killed by the great apes, one of which, Kala, took the infant and raised it as her own. Tarzan grew up in the jungle and educated himself with the books he found in his father's cabin.

It was after this point that the film company began to improvise. A sailor named Binns (George French) was added to befriend Tarzan and teach him English. Upon realizing that Tarzan was the Greystoke heir, Binns carried the news to England. An expedition was formed to go to Africa. Included were the foppish Greystoke nephew (Colin Kenny), his fiancee, Jane Porter, and her father, Professor Porter (Thomas Jefferson). Tarzan met Jane and they fell in love. The film concluded with their planning to return to England.

Newspaper advertisement announcing *Tarzan of the Apes.*

14

In one scene, a lion was supposed to be crawling through the window of Greystoke's cabin to devour the leading lady. Elmo grasped the beast by the mane and pulled it from the window. Although rather old and drugged, the lion really turned on the actor. And Elmo really killed him. He said afterwards, "When the lion jumped me, I stabbed him and he died. After a stunned moment, we continued shooting and I stepped on him to beat my chest. As my foot pressed down on him, the remaining air in his lungs escaped with a loud whoosh. I was already shaken and you should have seen me jump! That lion wound up as a lobby display when the picture opened on Broadway."

The eight-reeler directed by Scott Sidney opened at the Broadway Theatre in New York on January 27, 1918, and was a critical and financial smash. The *Chicago Journal* enthusiastically reported: "Wait till you see the apes and lions and elephants 'acting' in *Tarzan*." Elizabeth Lang Foy of *Film Magazine* wrote: "Most of us have read the story . . . that the filming of this most unusual tale was a worthy enterprise seems the unanimous verdict." Critic Mirilo, *Theatre Magazine*, summed it up: "This picture's fascination lies in its uniqueness."

*Tarzan of the Apes* was one of the first half dozen silent pictures to gross over a million dollars, making Parsons a wealthy man. Plans were immediately struck to complete a sequel before the year's end. When ERB objected, Parsons pointed out that National Film Corporation of America had purchased screen rights to *Tarzan of the Apes*. And if he, as producer, chose to film the book in two parts, that was his prerogative. There was nothing ERB could do.

The second film, *Romance of Tarzan*, was placed in general release in September, 1918. Lincoln and Enid Markey continued in their roles

Elmo Lincoln poses with foot on dead lion.

Enid Markey and Elmo Lincoln.

Elmo Lincoln in formal attire.

16

Colin Kenny, Enid Markey,
Thomas Jefferson, and Elmo
Lincoln in National's *Romance of
Tarzan*, 1918.

Enid Markey and Elmo Lincoln

Lord and Lady Greystoke in a special prologue filmed for *Son of Tarzan*.

Gordon Griffith as the youthful Tarzan.

Elmo Lincoln.

Lincoln with his ape-mother, Kala.

under the direction of Wilfred Lucas. The scenario by Bess Meredyth picked up after a brief synopsis of the first film. Just before sailing for England, they were attacked by natives and Tarzan was believed to have been killed. The relatives returned to England, and the Porters to their ranch near San Francisco. Very much alive and sporting a tuxedo, Tarzan followed Jane to her home and rescued her from bandits. Later she suspected him of taking up with another woman (Cleo Madison). Brokenhearted and disgusted with civilization, Tarzan returned to Africa. Realizing she was wrong, Jane set out after him.

The sequel did not receive raves like *Tarzan of the Apes* had, probably because it was not as painstakingly produced. A leading critic of the time, Louis Reeves Harrison, wrote in *Moving Picture World* that *"Romance of Tarzan* disregarded all that went to make up logic, sustained interest, vitality of theme and definite purpose . . . its sole reason for existence seems as an illustration for the book." "To take Tarzan from his jungle and make him the hero of a trashy story of the popular novel is a literary crime," spoke the *New York Times* (and so reviewed half of all future Tarzans); "as the uncivilized Apeman, Elmo is splendid, but as Tarzan in a dress suit—that is different."

*Motion Picture Magazine* offered the public's viewpoint of *Romance*: "There is an adventurous spirit about it which is entertaining." And the picture enjoyed much the same success as the original. Furthermore, two years later, Parsons reissued the two films on a double-bill that played to S.R.O. houses all over again.

With all these fabulous bookings, ERB reaped no more than his initial advance. In suing Parsons for royalties, he discovered that he was not the only one shorted. Scott Sidney, director of *Tarzan of the Apes,* filed suit against Parsons for the bonus he had been promised for completing the picture on schedule. The incorrigible Parsons came out on top again, making Burroughs leery of future film deals.

20

Colin Kenny, Thomas Jefferson, George French, Elmo Lincoln,
Enid Markey, and Bessie Toner in *Tarzan of the Apes,* 1918

Pollar with Charlie the elephant.

Pollar and Joe Martin the famous screen ape in *The Revenge of Tarzan*.

# 2 FIREMAN TO APEMAN

While the Lincoln epics were still playing, the competition for rights to a third Tarzan film began. ERB was determined not to let Parsons exploit another nickel out of his hero and entertained offers from several different companies. Believing their deal to be the best, ERB sold *The Return of Tarzan* to the Great Western Producing Company of the three Weiss brothers' Numa Pictures Corporation. Numa Pictures was an off-shoot of Weiss's Artclass Pictures Corporation, which had a reputation for shoddy and cheap products.

When Numa Pictures contacted Lincoln for another appearance as the Jungle Lord, he declined, saying that he was "already committed to do a number of serials for Universal." Numa replied that it was just as well because they needed a man who looked equally good in a tuxedo and lionskins. And Lincoln did not.

While in New York, one of the Weiss brothers was impressed by the size of a twenty-eight-year-old fireman, Joseph C. Pohler, who aspired to be an actor. A giant for his times, he was six feet

two and a half inches tall, weighed 215 pounds, and had a thirty-eight-inch waist. They changed his name to Gene Pollar and put him under contract for the lead in *The Return of Tarzan*, for which he was paid only $100 per week, plus wardrobe and traveling expenses.

Evelyn Fariss was to portray Jane but took ill when she learned that they were going to use real lions. Her sudden exit left the company without a Jane during the first month of production. Karla Schramm became Miss Fariss' replacement to play opposite Pollar.

Location shooting was done in New York, Florida, and Balboa, California, where fifty tons of palms, banana trees and all varieties of foliage were transplanted for the jungle sequences. The six-reeler directed by Harry Revier, featured Joe Martin, the famous screen ape, and Charlie the elephant, and boasted of using seven lions.

Only loosely based on ERB's book, Robert Saxmar's adaptation was contrived and inept. As always, the Weiss brothers compromised the film with poor production values to save on costs.

The story opened aboard an ocean liner bound for France. Tarzan, traveling with Jane, was answering a call for help from Countess de Coude (Estelle Taylor) who was being persecuted by her no-account brother, Rokoff (Armand Cortez). Rokoff then became Tarzan's enemy, swearing revenge. And Tarzan had an affair with the countess, was tossed overboard by Rokoff, ended up in North Africa, where he was captured. He escaped and went to Paris to search for Jane.

In Paris, Tarzan met with his friend, Paul D'Arnot (Franklin Coates). Then, after a duel with the countess' jealous husband (George Romain), Tarzan left for Africa and arrived in time to save Jane from a lion. She had been shipwrecked with Rokoff and his henchman (Walter Miller). In his element, Tarzan thwarted all threats from Rokoff.

The Numa production was sold in April, 1920, to Goldwyn Distribution Corporation, who cut it from nine reels to seven after a pre-release showing in New York. With Tarzan's popularity already established, *Return* was expected to do record business. But as a precautionary measure, since it featured a new star, the film was retitled *The Revenge of Tarzan* just two weeks prior to its opening on July 20. The title change was effected

Numa's *The Revenge of Tarzan*, 1920, with Gene Pollar and Karla Schramm.

One of the first shots of Tarzan riding an elephant.

Gene Pollar.

Pollar and a lion.

because of the "better exploitation possibilities it offers exhibitors . . . {it} is a better title in every way than the old one. It is stronger. It is more dramatic. It packs a punch." Goldwyn also felt that use of the word "return" led many to believe that this was a second run of an old picture.

Exhibitors, however, wanted to know where the title came into the story line. The general contention was that *Revenge* was a "fairly good picture but cannot compare with the first two Tarzans. Pollar is not an actor." One exhibitor in Nebraska

wrote to the *Exhibitors' Herald:* "Would have been a wonderful production if Elmo Lincoln had starred and used the pep he did in *Tarzan of the Apes.*" The *Moving Picture Herald* commented that "the novelty is lost in the latest release."

*Motion Picture News,* on the contrary, exclaimed: "The thrills are carefully staged and guaranteed, and the acting and directing are as good as need be." *Photoplay* agreed: *"Revenge of Tarzan* may be depended upon to duplicate the popular successes of the earlier picturizations of

Edgar Rice Burroughs' well-known novels. . . . By nature a muscular giant, his (Pollar's) performance adds realism to the well-staged production."

Regardless of how Pollar compared with Lincoln, *Revenge* was well received, pleasing the majority of cinema-goers. Pollar was the first to wear an over-the-shoulder and pants-like leopard skin.

On the strength of *Revenge's* returns, Universal Studios offered Pollar a two-year contract, at $350 a week, to make a series of Tarzan pictures for them. But Numa Pictures, which already owned Pollar would not release him unless Uni-

26

versal paid $800 a week, $100 of which Numa was willing to pass on to Pollar.

Disillusioned at being so close to fortune and being denied it, Pollar abandoned acting and returned to New York City, where he resumed his old job as a fireman.

Quitting the fire department in 1944, he became a purchasing agent for a retail store chain. He held that position for fourteen years before retiring to West Hollywood, Florida, for his health. At seventy-five, he is the oldest living Tarzan.

He still remembers his year in the picture business and likes to talk about it. "There's nothing that any of the other Tarzans did that I didn't do," Pollar said. "If you saw the movies back in those days, you know."

Karla Schramm and Ormond Cortez with Walter Miller, who later became one of the most popular players in serials, in *The Revenge of Tarzan.*

*The Son of Tarzan* opens at the Strand in New York.

# The SON OF TARZAN

They were alone together in the Jungle. Their daily life was just one thrilling adventure after another. You will love them both. Do not fail to attend the opening at the

**STRAND**

Opening
**NEW YEARS EVE**

# 3 TARZAN PLAYS SECOND FIDDLE

The death of William Parsons on September 28, 1919, made former treasurer Harry M. Rubey the new president of National Film Corporation and opened the way for new negotiations with ERB. During the successful run of *Revenge of Tarzan*, National paid Burroughs $20,000 for screen rights to *The Son of Tarzan* and promised him a percentage of the receipts. But when they couldn't get Pollar or Lincoln to star, and were reluctant to risk a new actor as the Apeman, they found themselves in a hole.

Producer David P. Howells, who had engineered the deal with ERB and controlled the property, decided they must abandon the format of the previous three films. They were in the heyday of the silent chapter plays and, he concluded, *The Son of Tarzan* should be a serial. And since he had no star, the production itself was to be featured in the publicity instead. "This picture," he told the press "will be an animal serial supreme with a special cast. It is to be no mad jumble of blood and thunder, nor a series of unrelated incidents intended to be a mystifying,

but will be a consistently constructed dramatic production."

On April 3, 1920, Rubey announced that western star Jack Hoxie, "who has become one of the leading serial stars through his work in *Lightning Bryce*, is to play the lead male role (that of Korak, Tarzan's son) and Lucille Rubey (Rubey's wife) will take the feminine lead. Production will begin immediately on an island in the South Pacific, with Harry Revier, who directed *Revenge of Tarzan*, directing. Over 300 apes, orangutangs, gorillas and chimpanzees have been contracted for."

As it turned out, everything in the above news release changed within a month, except the director. Backed by Jean Temple, casting directress, and producer Howells, Revier replaced Lucille Rubey with Kathleen May, who quickly relinquished the part to Manilla Martan. Jack Hoxie, who had been lukewarm on the film from the start, gave up the role of Korak to Kamuela C. Searle, a Hawaiian actor who had had an important role in Cecil B. DeMille's *Male and Fe-*

Kamuela Searle as Korak in *The Son of Tarzan*, 1920. Searle died from injuries suffered during the filming.

P. Dempsey Tabler beats his breast in National's *The Son of Tarzan*.

*male.* Gordon Griffith, who had played Tarzan as a boy in *Tarzan of the Apes*, was now to portray the son of Tarzan as a boy, replacing Kenneth Nordyke.

Revier then secured Karla Schramm to continue her portrayal of Jane from *Revenge*. "And Tarzan of the Apes was rather ably impersonated" by P. (Perce) Dempsey Tabler, a Tennessee athlete who had four seasons of light opera behind him. Born in 1880, Tabler, a six-foot, 190-pounder, was forty-one, had produced films, starred in several of Thomas H. Ince's Triangle productions, co-starred with William S. Hart in *Captive God*,

and had helped Bill Hodgkins found Paramount Studios. It was after a long absence from the screen that he agreed to replace House Peters as Tarzan. And since he was balding, he wore a wig—an ill-fitting one that fooled nobody.

The scant-physiqued, blue-eyed Tabler's acting career did not blossom anew with *Son of Tarzan* as he had hoped it might. Following the picture, he went into the advertising business in San Francisco and made his fortune there. He died in retirement at seventy-three.

Based on the book, the scenario, which was prepared by Roy Somerville and approved by

A rare wedding scene from *The Son of Tarzan* with P. Dempsey Tabler and Karla Schramm.

ERB, naturally focused on Tarzan's son, Jack (or Korak, which means killer in the language of the great apes), and his growth from boyhood to manhood. Playing away from Tarzan, the story began with Jack's being kidnapped from England by Tarzan's enemy, Ivan Paulovich (Eugene Burr). Korak escaped to the African jungle with the aid of Akut, Pualovich's trained ape. There he encountered Meriem (Mae Giraci as a girl; Manilla Martan as a young woman), a white girl who was held captive by a band of Arabs. With Akut, he freed her and a romance blossomed. Meriem, an heiress, was then sought by Paulovich and his

men for a ransom. She was protected by Korak and Tarzan, who turned up at his African estate with Jane. In one of the fights with Paulovich, Tarzan Tabler, who performed his own action work, broke several ribs.

A group photo of the three principals, Korak, Akut and Meriem, was used as a trademark in all advertising for the serial—on posters, special cut-outs, standees, slides, and heralds, and in lobby and window displays.

Before filming began, Searle spent four weeks in the desert in preparation for the role. According to Howells: "He wanted to harden and accustom

31

A still from *The Son of Tarzan* with a midget playing Akut the ape. Mae Giraci, Gordon Griffith.

Tabler and Eugene Burr.

himself to the life he will lead in the serial. His body has been sunburned to a dark brown, perfect for his part."

Production on *Son of Tarzan* started on May 15 at National's west coast studios, with a scheduled fifteen chapters of two reels each to be ready for fall release. A month later, Revier engaged Arthur J. Flaven, himself a well-known director, to assist in directing the fast-moving, slow-filming jungle picture. The final chapter was finished on January 27, 1921, each chapter having been released as completed. Cost of production was $106,000.

To provide a clear conception of the serial by audiences which might not have seen the earlier Tarzan films, director Revier arranged for a pictorial prologue to recount Tarzan's story from the first film to the point where *Son of Tarzan* began. Out of this prologue grew brief pictorial synopses which preceded each episode to relate the action that went before it. This innovation was picked up by the rest of the industry and has been used in serials to the present day.

The public followed the production of the serial closely, awaiting each chapter with zeal. And to encourage greater interest, Howells arranged with ERB to have the story of *Son of Tarzan* (as told in the picture) syndicated in newspapers across the country.

Howells also paid Norman Stuckey and Os-

Manilla Martan and Kamuela Searle.

Eugene Burr, Tabler, and Karla Schramm.

borne Tedman to write the music and lyrics, respectively, for the first Tarzan song, "Tarzan, my Jungle King." The four-page illustrated sheet music said: "Written and composed especially for *Son of Tarzan*, the World's Wonder Jungle Serial."

Then tragedy struck. While filming chapter fifteen, "An Amazing Denouncement," a sequence in the Village of Death called for Tantor the elephant, to rescue Korak, who was bound to a stake. The elephant, which was supposed to lower him to the ground gently after carrying him to safety, instead slammed him down so violently that the heavy stake, to which Searle was still tied, shattered. Searle later died of injuries sustained in the accident. Final scenes had to be shot with a double.

Although the accident was played down, it proved a major drawing card and people flocked to see the action that led up to the tragic incident.

The serial was noteworthy for its presentation of Tarzan's screen marriage to Jane Porter, performed in the first chapter by a minister. This was one of the few times Tarzan was married on film; other marriage scenes occur in *Tarzan and the Golden Lion* (1927) and *Tarzan the Mighty* (1928).

The *Exhibitors Herald* raved: "Best serial of all time . . . should have been twenty episodes or more instead of fifteen. Will be the greatest money-maker over the Christmas holidays." But, more realistically, *Motion Picture Magazine* pointed out that "even tho' good entertainment, *Son of Tarzan* could have been much improved with name actors."

P. Dempsey Tabler.

Action in *The Son of Tarzan*.

Candid shot on the set of *The Son of Tarzan*.

35

Poster for serial of *Adventures of Tarzan*.

Elmo Lincoln

#  THE RETURN OF THE ORIGINAL

Witnessing the early success of *Son of Tarzan*, the Great Western Producing Company, which was sponsored by Julius Stern and Oscar and Louis Jacobs, went to ERB for a Tarzan property to adapt as a chapter play. The author told them that he was not free to release any additional rights until the Weiss brothers of Numa Pictures Corporation had produced the remaining half of *Return of Tarzan*, the first part of which they had filmed and released as *Revenge of Tarzan*.

Although cool at first to any outside courting, Numa agreed to let Great Western produce a serial from their property when they learned that Great Western had Elmo Lincoln lined up as the star. The deal stipulated that Numa would then handle distribution of the film. Great Western apparently had been actively associated with Universal Film Manufacturing Company and for them had produced three successful Elmo Lincoln serials, *The Flaming Disk, Elmo the Mighty* and *Elmo the Fearless*, as well as a Lincoln-starred feature, *Under Crimson Skies*. And Lincoln, who had been unavailable to Numa for

*Revenge,* had consented to return to the role of Tarzan for Great Western.

Supporting Lincoln was tiny Louise Lorraine as Jane. She had been seen earlier as his leading lady in *Elmo the Fearless* and *The Flaming Disk*, in which she performed "almost as many dangerous stunts as the hero himself." A point made while selling *Adventures of Tarzan* to the public was that the green-eyed heroine "worked fearlessly with Numa, the lion, Tantor, the elephant, and Regent, the leopard, not permitting the use of double exposures." During production, Miss Lorraine celebrated her sixteenth birthday.

Filming began on January 1, 1921, at the Great Western west coast studios and moved later to Arizona on location for the desert scenes. The screenplay by Lillian Valentine and Robert F. Hill was based partially on *Return of Tarzan*, partially on *Tarzan and the Jewels of Opar,* and largely on invention. Much of the action centered on Tarzan's feud with Queen La of Opar (Lillian Worth), whose love he spurned, and his efforts to keep the bolshevik Rokoff (Frank Whitson)

CARL LAEMMLE presents

# UNIVERSAL SERIALS

the **cleanest, fastest** Serials ever screened

EDDIE POLO

EILEEN SEDGWICK

ELMO LINCOLN

ART ACORD

The bare-chested Lincoln in *Adventures of Tarzan.*

38

Huge six-foot poster for Elmo Lincoln's *Flaming Disc.*

## ELMO LINCOLN
### IN THE UNIVERSAL'S
### BIG SERIAL SENSATION
# "FLAMING DISK"

Miss Lorraine pets Tantor.

Elmo Lincoln

Lincoln protects Miss Lorraine.

and Clayton (Percy Pembroke), pretender to Tarzan's title as Lord Greystoke, from reaching Opar. Some cliffhangers in the first few episodes that kept audiences coming back: two lions leaping from above upon Tarzan from both sides; an active volcano cracking the earth, dropping Tarzan into a pit; sun worshippers about to sacrifice Tarzan; a struggle to the death on a sinking boat at night; and others equally as exciting.

Besides being largely responsible for the scenario, Hill also directed. Hill, whose reference to the serial as the "Tarzan of Tarzans" became a slogan used in advertising, stated his opinion at the completion of filming on August 13: "Specializing in the direction of chapter film plays for many years, I believe that in this serial I have finally achieved my dream of what should constitute this peculiar form of screen entertainment.

"Suspense, strength in episode climaxes, variance of locale, melodramatic situations and novelty of story are prime requsities for a successful serial. *Adventures of Tarzan* possesses all of these in abundance. I have directed Lincoln in many serials during the past five years, but have never seen him equal his performance as the Apeman of the jungles. He risked death many times in scenes with the various wild animals."

Hill's crisp direction, as much as Lincoln's fame as "the original Tarzan," was responsible for the serial's unprecedented success. The fact that Lincoln was returning to the role he popularized made *Adventures* one of the top four attractions of the year, equal to Rudolph Valentino's *The Four Horsemen of the Apocalypse*, Charlie Chaplin's *The Kid*, and Pola Negri's *Passion*.

When rumors circulated to the effect that *Adventures* was not a new production but a rehash of old films, Louis Weiss, secretary of the Serial Sales Corporation, stated emphatically that "all fifteen episodes of *Adventures of Tarzan* are brand new. Elmo Lincoln up to now has never appeared in a Tarzan serial of any kind. . . . Those interested in the production, including myself, naturally have a tremendous financial investment in this special production and I wish to nail now all rumors concerning this serial and to state that vigorous legal prosecution will follow any misleading statements regarding *Adventures of Tarzan*."

The *Exhibitors Herald's* review centered on the star: "Elmo Lincoln as Tarzan is too well known

A romantic still of Louise Lorraine and Elmo Lincoln in *Adventures of Tarzan*.

40

Elmo Lincoln in *Adventures of Tar-zan,* 1921.

Elmo Lincoln in *Adventures of Tarzan,* 1921.

Lincoln and the Oparians.

Greta Kemble Cooper as the stage Jane.

Photo Apeda

RONALD ADAIR

Brought over from London especially to play the part of Tarzan, in "Tarzan of the Apes," this actor was associated for several years, in his early stage days in England, with Bombardier Billy Wells, heavyweight boxer in a vaudeville sketch, knuckle fighting. For the last eighteen years he has been on the stage, with the exception of two years under Chas. B. Cochran as master of ceremonies at his championship boxing contests in London. He will have a strong character part in "The Right to Strike"

Tarzan in the theatre.

Relaxing on the set of *Adventures of Tarzan* Frank Merrill, a future Tarzan, stands behind Lincoln.

to theatre-goers to need further introduction. His red-blooded fights, staged in each episode, will evoke applause from the serial audience." And *Film Fun Magazine* blurbed: "There are enough wild animals introduced in each episode to keep the younger generation, which has shown a predilection for the serial form of entertainment, whooping her up."

For the purpose of exploiting and marketing the serial, the Adventures of Tarzan Serial Sales Corporation had been formed, with offices in New York under the auspices of the Weiss brothers. In those days, films were sold to territorial exchanges on a "states' rights" basis. The exchanges merely purchased the rights of distribution in different states. In a remarkable reception, the serial was sold in over fifty percent of available markets without use of a road man. And within three months after the completion date, *Adventures* was completely sold out in the United States, Canada, Australia, Central and Western Europe, Asia, South America, Central America, Mexico, the Indies, Pacific islands and the Philippines.

*Adventures* was Lincoln's farewell performance as the Apeman. Although his lion skin covered only his loins in the early chapters, censorship, which was then making itself heard loudly for the first time, forced him to cover his chest as well. Surprisingly unrestrictive where feminine nudity was concerned, the code apparently found the bare male torso objectionable. Later, with sound pictures, its blue-nosed views were reversed.

Also midway through the serial, Frank Merrill, who played an Arab guard and who would eight years later portray the Apeman, began doubling for the bulky Lincoln in acrobatic scenes and tree-climbing. Said Lincoln: "I was insured for $150,000. And when the insurance man saw me running around overhead, he threatened to cancel my policy." Reluctantly, Lincoln, who had always been proud of doing his own stuntwork, accepted Merrill to stunt for him.

Following *Adventures*, Lincoln's screen career began to diminish because he became typecast as the Apeman. His final silent performance was in a cheap Rayart serial, *King of the Jungle* (1927), in which he played a white hunter. During production on this serial, his old friend Gordon Standing was attacked and killed by a lion. Lincoln maintained that the accident could have been prevented. Disenchanted with film-making, he went to Mexico and invested in a mining development.

Twelve years later, Lincoln came back to Hollywood to play a part in Universal's *The Hunchback of Notre Dame* (1934). He continued doing small parts in scores of films like *The Iron Man, The Hollywood Story*, and others. He also appeared briefly in the Seal Brothers Circus, billed as "The Original Tarzan in Person."

An ironic bit of casting in 1949 brought him the small role of a jungle fisherman who crosses Tarzan's path in *Tarzan's Magic Fountain*. "The Apeman's character is degenerated," he said then. "They want to talk too much now." One of his final screen bows, shortly before his death on June 27, 1952, was in *Carrie*, which starred Sir Laurence Olivier and Jennifer Jones. He took pride in the scenes with Olivier, whom he admired greatly as an actor.

The incredible success of *Adventures of Tarzan* inspired a Broadway adaptation of *Tarzan of the Apes* at the Broadhurst Theatre in New York. London actor Ronald Adair, with eighteen years' stage experience, was imported by producer George Broadhurst to play the Apeman in 1921. "Greta Kemble Cooper made much of the role of Jane Porter," one critic said, but the critics raged at the play, insisting that it should have been left "to the films, as it is unsuitable behind the footlights."

Tarzan's failure in the legitimate theatre contrasted heavily with the box office success of the serial. Indeed, *Adventures* was recut and re-released in 1928 in a shortened feature version with sound effects, by the Weiss brothers' Artclass Film Company. It scored another success.

Lincoln and Mr. Burroughs.

Elmo Lincoln

46

# "ADVENTURES OF TARZAN"
## Starring ELMO LINCOLN

Here's a serial that everyone admits is a winner! A winner in every respect! Don't wait until it's too late. Book it—and book it quick!

Six Million People Have Read Edgar Rice Burrough's Tarzan Stories.

A Hundred Million Have Seen Elmo Lincoln As The Original Tarzan. Cash in on it!

THE WILD ANIMAL SERIAL SUPREME WITH HUNDREDS OF ANINALS INCLUDING

## JOE MARTIN

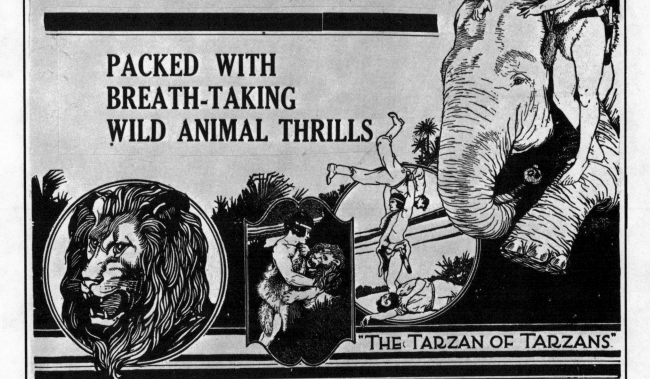

## PACKED WITH BREATH-TAKING WILD ANIMAL THRILLS

"THE TARZAN OF TARZANS"

# 5 A TARZAN IN THE FAMILY

Following *Adventures of Tarzan*, there were no Tarzan films undertaken until 1926, the longest lapse to occur between any two consecutive pictures in the series. The National Film Corporation ran into tax difficulties and had most of its assets confiscated; it did not outlive *Son of Tarzan*. And although the Weiss brothers continued as independent producers for several years, they never made another Tarzan picture.

Burroughs, anxious to see more of his hero on the screen, solicited and sold *Tarzan and the Golden Lion* to Edwin C. King, production head of Film Booking Offices (FBO), which later became RKO Radio Studios. The president of the company was financial wizard Joseph P. Kennedy, the late President Kennedy's father, who had purchased FBO a year earlier. He assigned *Golden Lion* to R-C pictures, who began production that August in the West San Fernando Valley area of Southern California, with James H. Pierce as the Apeman.

Big Jim Pierce, who was born August 8, 1900, had been an all-American center for Indiana Uni-versity, from which he graduated in 1921. For two years he coached in Arizona and took up acting in his spare time. In 1923, the six-foot-four 225-pounder won the lead in *The Deerslayer*, and after completing it, he stayed in California to coach at Glendale High School. At Glendale, the teams coached by Pierce included such later greats of filmdom as Duke Wayne, Bob Steele, and brothers Bob Livingston and Jack Randall.

After being noticed by a Paramount executive, Pierce was given the role of an aviator in their super-production of *Wings*. But before filming began, Pierce was discovered by ERB during a party at the author's Tarzana ranch. "There's Tarzan!" yelled the Master when he saw Pierce. "And then he proceeded to talk me into playing the Apeman," recalls Pierce. "He said I looked just like what he had always had in mind." Somewhat reluctantly, Pierce cancelled his agreement with Paramount, who, forced to find a replacement, gave the part to Gary Cooper.

"My salary as Tarzan," said Pierce, "was not much, but FBO assured me that it would sky-

Pierce as *The Deerslayer*, with Edna Murphy and Tom Tyler.

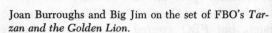

Joan Burroughs and Big Jim on the set of FBO's *Tarzan and the Golden Lion.*

50

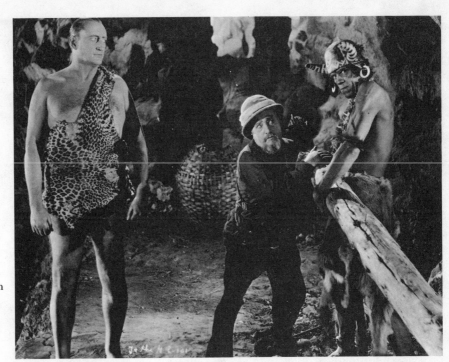

Boris Karloff in an early film role as an angry native.

Joan Burroughs and Big Jim Pierce today.

51

rocket once I galloped across the screen in a loincloth and the great American womanhood got a look at me. So with seventy-five dollars a week, I was off."

Halfway through the picture, the athletic actor began to wonder if he'd made the right decision. In one scene where he was chased by a lion, he had to climb hand-over-hand along a rope-vine stretched thirty-feet across a sixty-foot deep ravine. The studio-applied moss on the vine nearly caused him to lose his grip. "The whole thing was as much fun," he summed up later, "as running barefoot over rough, rocky ground can be."

Directed by famed action director J. P. Mc-Gowan, from a screenplay by William E. Wing, *Golden Lion* featured Dorothy Dunbar as Jane (now Tarzan's wife) and Edna Murphy as Flora Hawks, a blonde gal in love with the overseer (Harold Goodwin) of Tarzan's african estate. The plot involved an impersonation of the Apeman by Esteban Miranda (Fred Peters) and the search for a legendary city of diamonds. At the climax, Tarzan raced with his pet lion Jad-bal-ja to save Flora Hawks from being sacrificed to a lion-god. It was in this picture that Boris Karloff made his initial screen appearance, playing a bit part as Chief of the Waziri tribe.

This was the last silent Tarzan feature and adhered more closely to the book than any other production in the series. Although censors forced Jim to wear the over-the-shoulder leopard skins that had been introduced by Pollar, his loin coverings were briefer than his forerunner's had been. Big Jim also reverted to tennis shoes for some of the later outdoor scenes because his feet had been cut up pretty badly in the early action.

As filming neared completion, ERB wrote to Gordon Dorrance, a friend in Philadelphia; the letter, dated December 8, 1926, read: "I suggest you not miss the new Tarzan picture, *Tarzan and the Golden Lion*, just being completed by FBO here. I have seen some of the work during the making and also some of the rushes, and am convinced that it is going to be the greatest Tarzan picture ever made. We have found a man who really is Tarzan, and whom I believe will be raised to the heights of stardom."

ERB was wrong about the film. When *Golden Lion* premiered in February of 1927, it was popular with the public, but the critics lambasted it mercilessly. *Photoplay Magazine:* "This wins the hand-

From *Tarzan and the Golden Lion.*

Pierce and Edna Murphy.

Pierce with Harold Goodwin, Edna Murphy, Dorothy Dunbar, and D'Arcy Corrigan in *Tarzan and the Golden Lion*.

Jim Pierce.

Pierce and Joan Burroughs Pierce

Jim Pierce.

Pierce during the early days of the Tarzan Radio Show.

embroidered toothpick as being the worst picture of the month. The former Tarzans were enjoyable. But this is filled with such improbabilities that it becomes ridiculous." The *Motion Picture Exhibitor* appraised it less emotionally, acclaiming it "profitable, although overdone, and a weakly exciting addition to the series." Kindest by far was *Film Daily:* "Pretty far-fetched; but a new order of thrills and atmosphere that might prove distinctly attractive."

Pierce himself was disappointed: "Because of

55

Mr. Burroughs discusses *Tarzan and the Golden Lion* with director, J. P. McGowan.

poor direction, terrible story treatment and putrid acting, the opus was a stinkeroo. I emerged with nothing to show for my strenuous effort except being typecast as Tarzan. I was out of a job." Ironically, Paramount gave him a small part in *Wings* after he finished *Golden Lion*. But once *Golden Lion* was released, casting directors knew him as "Tarzan" Pierce and wouldn't give him a break. Wisely, Pierce returned to coaching high school teams, playing bit parts on the side.

In the meantime, Pierce courted Burroughs' only daughter, Joan, whom he had met at that first party. They had become very close during the *Golden Lion* production, and they were married on August 8, 1928. As a wedding present,

Papa Burroughs wrote Big Jim as Tarzan into the screen rights to an unpublished Tarzan manuscript in an option he gave an independent producer. This option later presented quite a problem for ERB.

Burroughs, strangely enough, always regarded Pierce as the perfect Tarzan. Consequently, when he organized the "Tarzan radio act" in 1932, he asked his daughter and son-in-law to play the Apeman and mate over the air. Altogether, they recorded 364 fifteen-minute episodes of the successful radio serial, which by 1934 had been sold in every state, South America, and Western Europe.

Pierce abandoned the series to play King Thun,

56

the Lion-Man, in Universal's history-making serial, *Flash Gordon* (1936), which starred the 1933-vintage Tarzan veteran, Buster Crabbe. Then drifting into westerns, he was featured in *Zorro's Fighting Legion* (1938), a Republic serial with Reed Hadley. He went on to support such stars as Tex Ritter, Tim McCoy, and Bob Livingston.

He finally hung up his guns, and with them his film career, in the forties to devote more time to his booming real estate agency in the San Fernando Valley. An excellent pilot, Jim was very active in the war years with the organization of the National Airmen's Reserve, Inc., at the Metro-politan Airport in Van Nuys. This reserve group was the foundation for today's Air National Guard.

Semi-retired today, Jim Pierce and his wife reside in Apple Valley, California, adjacent to the famous Apple Valley Golf Course. Both avid golfers, they spend a lot of time on the green. And as in the past eighteen years, Jim is still active in Rotary International. The Pierces take great pride and enjoyment in their five grandchildren, Kasey (one), Kathy (three), Kelly (five), Brooke (two) and Jim IV (six), "who may someday play Tarzan, too," wagers Big Jim.

Merrill with Bobby Nelson as Boy.

Merrill tames a crocodile.

# 6 FADEOUT OF THE SILENT APEMAN

At about the same time that Jim Pierce was at work on *Tarzan and the Golden Lion* and Elmo Lincoln filmed *King of the Jungle*, ex-stuntman Frank Merrill, who had doubled for Lincoln in 1921, starred in *Perils of the Jungle* for Weiss Brothers Artclass Productions. This chapter, dealing with the transition to the talking films, is Frank Merrill's story.

After the critical chastisement given *Golden Lion*, FBO refrained from making a sequel. Instead, the Apeman was given a new home at Universal Studios, who recalled the days when their Elmo Lincoln serials were big box office, no matter how shabbily reviewed.

Consequently, Universal, the first major production company to become involved in the series, paid ERB an undisclosed sum of money to let them make a serial from *Jungle Tales of Tarzan*. With the aid of directors Jack Nelson and Ray Taylor, Ian McClosky Heath wrote a shooting

continuity titled after the book, but later called *Tarzan the Mighty*.

For the role of Tarzan, Universal contracted the action king of serials, Joe Bonomo, who was distinguished for his strength and stuntwork. A great deal of publicity and exploitation went out on Bonomo as "the greatest of all Tarzans." But towards the end of another picture, *Perils of the Wild*, the human dynamo fractured his left leg and severely injured his sacro-iliac in a stunt and cancelled his commitment.

During the replacement-casting session that followed, director Nelson remembered the muscular actor he had worked with on *Perils of the Jungle* a year before and called him. The six-foot, 200-pound Merrill modestly accepted the offer and reported for work the next morning, April 12, 1928.

His co-star was Natalie Kingston, who played Mary Trevor instead of Jane, yet ended up as his mate anyway. Mary and her young brother Bobby

Merrill with Bobby Nelson and Natalie Kingston in *Tarzan the Mighty*.

Merrill and gorilla in *Tarzan the Mighty*.

Natalie Kingston pleads with Merrill for the life of Al Ferguson.

(Bobby Nelson) were castaways befriended by Tarzan. Most of the action in the serial consisted of recounting Tarzan's origin and a series of clashes between the Apeman and Black John (Al Ferguson), the ruler of an African village of pirates' descendants. When Tarzan's uncle, Lord Greystoke (Lorimer Johnson), arrived, looking for the family heir, Black John passed himself off as the lost relative. His scheme was successful and he was about to wed Mary Trevor in England when Tarzan appeared to set things straight and wed Mary himself.

Originally scheduled for twelve episodes, *Tarzan the Mighty* was so successful that Universal extended it to fifteen, with shooting concluding on October 28, 1928. Much of its success was rightly attributed to the powerful Merrill, whose daredevil stunts kept the serial's pace at a fast clip.

Before films, Merrill had been a gymnast and had won fifty-eight National, Southern California and Los Angeles metropolitan championships on Roman rings, high bars and for rope climbing. He

was national gymnastic champ from 1916 to 1918. Drawing on his skills for the serial, he conceived Tarzan's vine-swinging techniques. In one scene Merrill swings through the trees holding Natalie Kingston in one arm, a feat made possible by a loop he fashioned on a vine-disguised rope for a safer grasp.

And although the rope snapped under their combined weight in the middle of the swing and they (fortunately, unhurt) had to do it again, Merrill's innovations led the way to the screen Tarzan of the thirties. When MGM three years later began production on their Tarzan series with Johnny Weissmuller, they held several showings of Merrill's work to study his vine-swinging and rope-climbing.

Merrill's superb physique was an important factor in the serial's fantastic reception. He, even more than Elmo Lincoln, seemed perfectly suited for the part. When a friend of his learned of a physical culture contest being held in England, he entered Merrill's photograph without his knowledge. Merrill was later astonished to discover that he was second runner-up for the title of "World's Most Perfectly Developed Man," from which publicity further boosted attendance of *Tarzan the Mighty*. It was a shame that Merrill was subjected to shoulder-length leopard skins because his body, which was more splendid than any other silent Tarzan's, should have been displayed. Like Lincoln, he wore a headband.

In those early Depression days, *Tarzan the Mighty* yielded so much money for Universal

Merrill in Universal's *Tarzan the Tiger*, 1929. Lillian Worth as Queen La of Opar.

that they quickly followed it with a sequel, *Tarzan the Tiger*. They assigned their top serial director, Henry McRae, to the production for which Ian McClosky Heath wrote an adaptation of *Tarzan and the Jewels of Opar*.

Natalie Kingston continued as the heroine, but this time as Jane. The villain was Al Ferguson again, posing as a friendly scientist who sells Jane into slavery after Tarzan's African estate is raided by Arabs. The rest of the plot was an oft-repeated Burroughs formula. Tarzan Merrill, as the result of a blow on the head in chapter three, not only lost his memory, but couldn't distinguish between friends and foes for the next ten chapters. A second blow in chapter thirteen brought him back to his senses and left him two episodes in which to best the villain, secure the jewels of Opar, and rescue Jane.

Released an episode at a time from October, 1929, to February, 1930, *Tarzan the Tiger* enjoyed the same popular favor as *Tarzan the Mighty*, and is of particular interest in that it was the only Tarzan film to be made in both silent and semi-sound versions. The "sound" version was a hurried attempt to capitalize on the "coming of the talkie." It consisted of a crudely orchestrated musical score, sound effects, and a few roughly lip-synchronized lines on a record.

On that record was the first Tarzan yell, another innovation of the fifth screen Apeman. Merrill, who thus became simultaneously the last silent and the first "talkie" Tarzan, was always proud of the fact that he did his own stunts and devised the original ape-call.

Tarzan's famous yell as we know it today was a product of MGM's sound department and was not perfected until 1934. They laid four different sound tracks (the bleat of a camel, howl of a hyena, growl of a dog, pick of a violin's G-string) over Johnny Weissmuller's yodel, which was played at a slower speed and an octave higher. They timed it so that each of the sounds played a fraction of a second after the preceding one. Weissmuller (and, later, Lex Barker) learned to imitate the eerie guttural sound, and his voice replaced the recording. It is Weissmuller's yell that was heard on NBC-TV's *Tarzan* series, because star Ron Ely hadn't been able to master it.

Merrill's fame was intense and shortlived. With *Tarzan the Mighty*, he more or less finished his film career. They had considered a third film

Al Ferguson menaces Merrill and Miss Kingston.

GREATER THAN 'TARZAN THE MIGHTY'!

**TARZAN THE TIGER**
with FRANK MERRILL and NATALIE KINGSTON
THE ORIGINAL TARZAN
EDGAR RICE BURROUGHS

called *Tarzan the Terrible*, after ERB's book of the same title, but it was decided that Merrill's voice was unsuitable for the talkies and it was never made. Merrill, himself, was almost ready to retire from movies anyway. On his personal appearance tours in his leopard skin, he realized the influence he had on kids and decided to devote his life to them. By way of Tarzan he found his true vocation. For years he worked with kids for the Los Angeles city administration, on the Parks Commission and as a recreation director.

After retiring in 1963, following a serious operation, he donated his services to the YMCA as gym instructor.

On February 12, 1966, Frank Merrill, seventy-two, passed away.

In late life, he liked to talk about his stint as the Jungle Lord. He felt that "the character of Tarzan was destroyed when they put street clothes on him. Burroughs had intended him to stay in the jungles." When asked if he had read any of the Tarzan books, he confessed that he hadn't.

Frank Merrill and Natalie Kingston in Universal's *Tarzan the Mighty*.

Lobby card.

ADVENTURE PICTURES Present

**TARZAN THE TIGER**
with FRANK MERRILL THE ORIGINAL TARZAN
AND THE BEAUTIFUL NATALIE KINGSTON
FROM THE STORY "TARZAN AND THE JEWELS OF OPAR"
by
EDGAR RICE BURROUGHS

Directed by
HENRY McRAE

BOOK TWO
# THE TALKIES

The advent of sound in moving pictures was a long time coming, actually in the developing stages over fifty years. Men like Thomas Edison had early visions of the silent screen learning to speak. From experiments with crude devices that attempted to co-ordinate sound with pictures by use of ear tubes and roughly lip-synchronized records grew Warner Brothers' Vitaphone talking pictures. The release of *The Jazz Singer* in October, 1927, in which Al Jolson actually sang and spoke from the screen, signaled the beginning of the end for the silent era.

By 1930, with few exceptions, silent films were a thing of the past. The old Hollywood star system crumbled, and new actors and actresses with fine speaking voices were demanded. Stage experience became a must.

This early wave of talkies electrified moviegoers. They sat for hours on end in darkened theatres, enthralled and fascinated by the wonder of it all.

"Gee, talking pictures! What will they think of next?"

# 7 A LONG REIGN BEGINS

In early 1931 Metro-Goldwyn-Mayer Studios revelled in the success of their African-filmed *Trader Horn*, a picture featuring Edwina Booth, a blonde newcomer, as a white goddess among savages, and Duncan Renaldo and Harry Carey as white hunters. Apparently, a great deal of excess jungle footage remained from the production. "Why not use it for a Tarzan film?" came the suggestion from Ralph Rothmund, the general manager of Edgar Rice Burroughs, Incorporated.

Acting on studio czar Louis B. Mayer's instructions, Metro's "boy wonder" production head, Irving Thalberg, obtained exclusive rights from Burroughs to a Tarzan property with an option for an additional one. Following initial announcements that MGM was preparing the "biggest, most colossal jungle epic seen to date," William S. Van Dyke, the studio's ace director, who had been a protégé of D. W. Griffith and had earned his spurs on *Trader Horn*, began his search for the new Apeman.

"What I want is a man who is young, strong, well-built, reasonably attractive, but not neces-

sarily handsome, and a competent actor," said Van Dyke when the hunt was on. "The most important thing is that he have a good physique. And I can't find him." Van Dyke tested hundreds of actors, college men, and athletes, without success. He dismissed Charles Bickford with "Not young enough," Joel McCrea with "Never heard of him," Johnny Mack Brown with "Not tall enough;" and as for Clark Gable, "He has *no body*," shrugged Van. "I want someone like Jack Dempsey, only younger. Tom Tyler is the best so far, but he's not muscular enough."

When Douglas Fairbanks, Sr., heard of the role requirements he suggested that Van Dyke consider Herman Brix, a six-foot-three, 212-pound All-American football star from Washington University who had won the shot-put championship in the 1928 Olympic Games in Amsterdam. After seeing Brix, Van was all set to sign him. At the time Brix was working on his first picture, *Touchdown*, at Paramount, but during the initial week of production, he broke his shoulder. Uncertain of Brix's recovery period, Van Dyke shied away.

Weissmuller and second wife, Lupe Velez.

In the meantime, screen-writer Cyril Hume, who was working on the scenario for *Tarzan the Apeman,* was staying at the same hotel as Johnny Weissmuller, the 1924 and 1928 Olympic swimming champion. Impressed by Weissmuller's graceful physique upon seeing him in the hotel pool, Hume invited him to meet Van Dyke and

Bernard Hyman, the producer of *Apeman,* to discuss the Tarzan role. During the interview with the director and producer, Weissmuller was unexpectedly stripped to his shorts and offered the part without even a screen test.

But Weissmuller couldn't move quite that fast. He had a contract with BVD to represent their swimming trunks and underwear. Weissmuller's coach, William "Big Bill" Bachrach, had arranged the deal with BVD when Weissmuller married

Tarzan, Jane, and Cheetah.

Bobbe Arnst, a petite singer-dancer, in Miami in 1930. The five-year contract paid $500 a week but had cost Weissmuller his amateur athletic standing, ending his fantastic nine-year swimming career.

Peter Johnny Weissmuller, who was born in Windber, Pennsylvania, on June 2, 1904, had been a scrawny, sickly kid. Upon the advice of a doctor, he took up swimming to build himself up in order to fight off a withering sickness. Under the patient guidance of "Big Bill" Bachrach, the lanky weakling developed into a six-foot-three 190-pound champion athlete who retired undefeated with five Olympic gold medals, sixty-seven world and fifty-two national titles. During his career, he had broken 174 individual records, helped break twenty-one relay records and held every free-style record from 100-yards to the half-mile. Twenty years later, in 1950, he was named the greatest swimmer of the past half-century by world sportswriters in an Associated Press poll.

Yes, the role of Tarzan appealed to Weissmuller, but BVD, who stood between him and the MGM lion, said "No!" They had intervened in Johnny's film career two years earlier when he appeared briefly in Paramount's *Glorifying the American Girl*. He was supposed to be Adam, wearing only a fig leaf, while standing atop a fake world holding Mary Eaton as Eve on his shoulders. Thinking that the fact that Johnny wore only a fig leaf would hurt swim suit sales, BVD forced Paramount to cut all of the scene, except for long shots in which Weissmuller was undistinguishable. And, as far as BVD was concerned, Weissmuller was too valuable to be released to Metro, or to anyone. But Metro, determined to have him, sent over a team of lawyers to work out an agreement.

Finally, after lengthy negotiations the deal was

Weissmuller, Maureen O'Sullivan, and C. Aubrey Smith.

Weissmuller stands over Miss O'Sullivan, C. Aubrey Smith, and Neil Hamilton.

closed. In return for Johnny's freedom, Metro agreed to let BVD photograph all their contract players in BVD swim suits, including stars like Greta Garbo, Joan Crawford, Jean Harlow, and even Marie Dressler! Johnny's contract with MGM was for seven years at six-month option intervals, beginning at $500 a week, with raises up to $2,000 weekly or more within the given period.

In the publicity buildup for the film, Weissmuller was billed as the "only man in Hollywood who's natural in the flesh and can act without clothes." Van Dyke had complained earlier that "most actors without clothes are undressed rather than naked and are too self-conscious to act naturally."

For Jane, Thalberg chose a lovely twenty-year-old actress from Ireland, Maureen O'Sullivan. Fair, dark-haired, curvaceous, delicate, and as feminine as Weissmuller was masculine, she proved the perfect mate for the moody, uncommunicative Tarzan.

Hume's screenplay bore little resemblance to ERB's *Tarzan of the Apes* and omitted all reference to Tarzan's origin, concentrating instead on the romantic interest between the jungle man and the English girl. Filmed in five months in the Toluca Lake area of North Hollywood, the story began with Jane Porter arriving in Africa to join her father (C. Aubrey Smith) and his young partner, Harry Holt (Neil Hamilton), who are about to leave their trading post in search of ivory at the legendary elephant burial ground. When Tarzan comes upon their safari, he whisks Jane away to his tree-top abode where the immortal line by British playwright and actor Ivor Novello, "Tarzan—Jane" (not "Me Tarzan—you Jane," as it is commonly misquoted) was delivered.

At the climax of the picture, a tribe of pygmies captured the safari and began lowering their captives one by one to a giant gorilla in a pit. Tarzan arrived with a herd of elephants, which wrecked the village while he fought the gorilla. Afterwards, a wounded elephant showed the way to the burial ground. When Jane's injured father died, she sent Holt back to civilization alone, having elected to stay with Tarzan, presumably in a common-law marriage.

Hume and Novello as much as Van Dyke and Weissmuller shared the responsibility for the ma-

Weissmuller and Mr. Burroughs,
1932.

Weissmuller leaps into the gorilla pit.

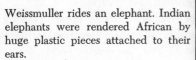

Weissmuller rides an elephant. Indian
elephants were rendered African by
huge plastic pieces attached to their
ears.

jor surgery on ERB's champion in this picture. It was in this film that Tarzan changed from an intelligent, well-spoken English lord into an unintelligible white ape. The sophistication and fine manners with which Lincoln, Pollar, Tabler, and others of the silent era moved about in Parisian and London circles was lost, nonexistent to Metro's crude jungle man, who was on the same level with beasts. And much to Burroughs' dismay, Weissmuller's portrayal became the prototype for later Tarzans. Years later, when asked the secret of his success, Weissmuller said simply, "My grunt."

Just a few weeks into production on *Apeman*, a crisis arose. Sol Lesser, an independent producer,

announced preparations on a Tarzan film. It seems that the rights to a Tarzan picture that ERB had optioned to an independent producer in 1928 had found their way into Lesser's hands. The date for payment required to be made to Burroughs, at the time production commenced, had lapsed, but Jules Goldstone, a lawyer, told Lesser that legally the contract was enforceable. The requirement under law was that the party in question (ERB) had to notify the one who was in default and no such notification had been given.

"The thing to do," recalls Lesser, "was to tender the payment of ten thousand dollars called for. So I gave the money to Mr. Goldstone, who went to Burroughs' Malibu home. When Mr. Burroughs answered the door, Jules gave him the ten thousand-dollar bills. 'What's this for?' asked Burroughs. To which Goldstone replied that it was payment for the rights to make a Tarzan picture which he had optioned five years before and which we had acquired. Burroughs threw the money back and said the contract had lapsed. But Goldstone merely retrieved the money and returned it to Burroughs."

Lesser then filed suit in declaratory relief for the courts to decide if the contract was valid. When the decision was delivered in Lesser's favor, Metro lawyers besieged him to delay production of any Tarzan film until after *Tarzan the Apeman* had been released. For a nominal fee, Lesser was persuaded. This made a big hit with Burroughs, who was in a spot because in his contract with MGM he alleged that there were no outstanding rights. Although at odds in the beginning, Lesser and ERB became lifelong friends and worked out a five-picture contract, at the rate of one per year.

When *Tarzan the Apeman* was unleashed on the public in March of 1932, it was an immediate sensation, justifying the million-dollar production costs. One of the top ten box office hits of the year, it ranked with pictures like *Hell Divers, Grand Hotel, Mata Hari, Dr. Jekyll and Mr. Hyde, Arrowsmith,* and *Shanghai Express.*

Critical acclaim proportionately accompanied the film's financial returns. The cynical critic, Francis Birrell, of the London magazine *The New Statesman and Nation,* wrote: "For an hour and three-quarters (a long stretch for a film) the eye is continually delighted, the nerves unceasingly harassed. Armies of elephants, torments of monkeys, prides of lions sweep across the screen . . . *Tarzan* has a hundred percent entertainment value, and gains enormously over such pictures as *Trader Horn* by never pretending to provide accurate information. It is just a terrific piece of gusto in the romantic manner."

"However credible or interesting Tarzan may be on the printed page," said Thornton Delehanty in the *New York Evening Post,* "I doubt very much if he emerges in such splendor as he does in the person of Johnny Weissmuller, who makes his bow to the movie-going public. And as Tarzan he will probably remain bowing through a whole series of these pictures, even tho the public may clamor to see him in Clark Gable roles. There is no doubt that he possesses all the attributes, both physical and mental, for the complete realization of this son-of-the-jungle role. With his flowing hair, his magnificently proportioned body, his catlike walk, and his virtuosity in the water, you could hardly ask anything more in the way of perfection.

"Single-handed he attacks lions and tigers; he

Tarzan learns to count.

A romantic interlude.

leaps off a tree onto the back of a waterbuck and throws it with one twist of the neck; he makes a herd of elephants as subservient as a troupe of trained fleas."

"But the most vital statistic of all," insisted Katherine Albert in *Photoplay Magazine*, "is the fact that a lad who had never been in a picture before, who had been interested in nothing but swimming all his life, and who frankly admits he can't act, is the top-notch heart-flutterer of the year."

MGM, cautious about picking up Weissmuller's first option, did so only after they saw his large-scale acceptance by the public. He was the biggest new star of 1932, mentioned in the same breath with Gary Cooper, Jean Harlow, Clark Gable, and all the big names. And now that Johnny was one of the family, the studio began to make demands of him. Seeing he was a big favor-

ite with the girls, they told him to get rid of his wife. She stood in the way of his career, they said. To soften the blow on Bobbe, Metro paid her $10,000. "I can go back to singing," she told Johnny, "and besides, it *is* a lot of money."

MGM immediately made plans for a sequel, exercising its contractual option with ERB. A twelve-acre jungle and a thirteen-million-gallon asphalt-bottomed lake were specially built on the studio back lots. A zoo was also initiated in anticipation of a possible series.

But first, Weissmuller went on the road to support *Apeman* with personal appearances. While in New York, he met Lupe Velez, a fiery Latin singer-actress-comedienne, who also was a Metro

74

contract player. Although the studio had nixed Johnny's first marriage, they saw no objection to his building a relationship with Lupe, as long as it got good publicity.

Following a stormy, well-publicized courtship, they were married in Nevada in 1933. Although violently in love, they were just as violently mismatched. He was a day person who liked to get to bed early; she was a night person who didn't need sleep. She taught him to smoke and drink and how to party. He wanted children, but she didn't. Both were short-tempered and emotional; they were always fighting, separating and making up. Neighbors claimed their house sounded like a battlefield.

Eventually, they split up for good and were divorced in 1938. Six years later, Lupe, who never remarried, committed suicide. Johnny couldn't believe it at first. Then he blamed himself as being partly at fault.

Rare still of crocodile fight scene which appeared in five
different films

Crabbe absorbed in his work

# ⑧ THE LION MAN VS. THE APEMAN

Once *Tarzan the Apeman* was released, Lesser was not obliged to wait any longer. Armed with his five-picture contract, he moved quickly to produce his first Tarzan film. But in checking the contract he purchased through Goldstone, he discovered a clause stipulating that Pierce was to play the Apeman. At the time, Big Jim was recording the Tarzan radio serial and could easily have made the picture. But Lesser, regarding Pierce as part of the silent era, wanted Weissmuller or a sensual athlete like him for his film. The massive ex-football hero was not the image he sought.

Lesser pointed this out to Burroughs, who shrugged and said that it was between him and Pierce. "But if he insists on doing the part," Lesser reasoned, "I would have to treat it as a comedy, because he's the wrong type. And if I did, the character of Tarzan would be lost." ERB retorted that it wouldn't be any worse than what they did at Metro. "Besides," the author added, "I don't think anything could hurt the Tarzan character. It's survived a helluva lot."

With ERB's apparent sanction, Lesser engaged Corey Ford to do a travesty in which Jane assumed the masculine role and was the strong one in the family. She would do things like boosting Tarzan up a tree. It was actually written that way, but Lesser, unhappy with the treatment, approached Pierce with a deal. He offered him $5,000 and promised him a screen test at MGM if he would step aside. Still a bit naive about the business, Pierce accepted. When he reported to Metro for the pre-arranged screen test, he was given a Shakespearean soliloquy to read. Admittedly an athlete rather than an actor, Pierce felt they were laughing up their sleeves about the so-called "test." He never mastered Shakespeare, nor did he ever work for MGM.

Now that Pierce was out, Lesser was free to cast whomever he wanted. Since Metro wouldn't consider loaning Weissmuller to the producer for

77

an independent Tarzan picture, he checked around Hollywood to see who was available. During Lesser's search, Paramount released a Tarzan-inspired film called *King of the Jungle,* which was the story of Kaspa, the Lion Man. Although based on Charles T. Stoneham's novel, *The Lion's Way,* it would have been difficult for Paramount to have produced a film more similar to Metro's epic without calling their hero Tarzan. Quite an elaborate production, *King of the Jungle* was backed by a huge publicity campaign about their star, Buster (Clarence Linden) Crabbe, being the 1932 Olympic swimming champion in the 400-meter free style event.

Curiously enough, the twenty-three-year-old Crabbe, a University of Southern California graduate, had been one of the local college men tested for *Tarzan* in 1931. "But the test wasn't fair," grumbled the Lion Man then. "I was working for Columbia on a college picture at the time, called *That's My Boy,* and Metro came out to the studio and grabbed a quick group test and didn't give any of us a chance."

Paramount, who sought a husky athlete-actor to play their Lion Man, paid a bit more attention to Crabbe. And after narrowing the screen tests down to five, they had a group of studio secretaries select the winner. Crabbe was the unanimous choice.

In preparation for the role, Crabbe's high-pitched voice was lowered to a mild growl by a Paramount voice teacher. Crabbe's sincere cooperation and hard work earned him a one-year contract before the picture was finished. The advertising was geared to push him as Weissmuller's rival.

Appropriately, both he and Johnny were Olympic swimmers and had outstanding physiques. Although Johnny was two inches taller and ten pounds heavier, Crabbe's chest was four inches bigger and he had wider shoulders, too.

Having been swimming pals for a number of years, Crabbe and Weissmuller thought the heavily publicized rivalry humorous. On the other hand, producer Lesser took it in earnest and became convinced that Crabbe was the Tarzan for him. He contracted Crabbe on a loan-out from Paramount for *Tarzan the Fearless,* which was shot in the San Fernando Valley as *Tarzan the Invincible,* but was retitled.

Crabbe's co-star was Jacqueline Wells, an obscure blonde actress, who has since become famous as Julie Bishop. In an effort to be somewhat different from Metro's version, Lesser cast her as Mary Brooks instead of Jane Porter, and she became Tarzan's mate at the film's end. Playing it safe, he signed Robert Hill, famed veteran of the Elmo Lincoln serials, to direct.

Weissmuller rides the elephant for MGM's *Tarzan and his Mate,* 1934

Weissmuller with Rod La Rocque,
Neil Hamilton, and Miss O'Sullivan

The same shot with Paul Cavanaugh replacing La Rocque

Buster Crabbe in Principal Productions' *Tarzan the Fearless*,
1933

79

One fidelity to the MGM film that Lesser insisted on was that Crabbe play Tarzan á la Weissmuller, and not as Burroughs wrote him. Metro's interpretation of Burroughs' self-educated Apeman as a simple primitive seemed successful, and Lesser remained faithful to it through the twenty-six years he was connected with the series.

Based ever so lightly on the characters created by ERB, the screenplay was fashioned by Basil Dicky and George Plympton, with dialogue by Walter Anthony. The somewhat disconnected plot found Tarzan aiding Mary Brooks in the search for her father (E. Alyn Warren), who had been studying ancient tribes and had fallen into the hands of "the people of Zar, god of the Emerald Fingers." The villainy was supplied by the high priest of Zar (Mischa Auer), his right-hand man, Abdul (Frank Lackteen) and two unscrupulous safari guides, Jeff (Philo McCullough) and Nick (Mathew Betz). After Tarzan rescued everyone from the clutches of the high priest, he took Mary Brooks to his cave, where he grunted approval of her. Here *Tarzan the Fearless* ended abruptly,

Crabbe rescues Jacqueline Wells

An ape protects Crabbe from Zarian warriors

Rare shot of Weissmuller atop Mary the rhinoceros

with none of the villains dealt with in final terms.

Uniquely, the picture was released by Principal Distributing Corporation on August 11, 1933, as both a 71-minute feature and a serial, the first chapter of which was an hour long and somewhat nebulously complete in itself. Lesser's intent was for exhibitors to follow the feature-chapter with eight additional two-reel installments, or they could run the picture strictly as a serial in twelve episodes. Unfortunately, many theatres just ran the feature part without the last eight chapters. And since the feature left many things unresolved, it, being appraised as a complete film, received poor reviews.

London's *The Nation* magazine, which had applauded *Tarzan the Apeman*, chastised *Tarzan the Fearless*. William Troy wrote: "If Mr. Burroughs' Tarzan books are not beyond the reach of an eight-year-old mind, the movie versions of them may be said to reduce the age limit by three or four years. In fact, even an intelligent child of five might find something embarrassing in the manner in which an unfortunate young athlete named Buster Crabbe is required to jump about from tree to tree, caress synthetic Hollywood apes, and make hideously inhuman noises."

The consensus was uncannily uniform. *Photoplay Magazine* ruled that "the story is as disjointed and inane as Tarzan stuff usually is, but Buster *is* decorative. . . ." And New York critic Aaronson, of the *Motion Picture Herald*, left no doubt as to his opinion: "It is splendid youngster material."

Just prior to the film's release, Buster Crabbe married Adah Virginia Held, his college sweetheart. After the honeymoon, he decided to give himself one year to make good as an actor; otherwise, it was back to USC to study law. Paramount gave him a new contract and put him in a series of Zane Grey westerns. His action performance in these oaters brought him to Universal's attention, and they wooed him away from Paramount for their spectacularly successful *Flash Gordon, Red Barry* and *Buck Rogers* serials (1936-40). Then in 1940, it was back to westerns for a long string of Billy the Kid pictures with Al "Fuzzy" St. John as his sidekick.

Following World War II, Crabbe, who had appeared between films in Billy Rose's "Aquacade," at the New York World's Fair with Weissmuller and other swimming stars like Eleanor

Weissmuller and Cheetah perplexed by Jane's formal attire

Weissmuller receives first aid from the apes

Holm, formed his own "Aqua Show" and toured the world. Then returning to films, he made some serials for Columbia, including one as T'hunda, a comic strip jungle hero, in *King of the Congo* (1951). More westerns followed, several water shows, and a long-run, now syndicated, TV show called *Captain Gallant of the Foreign Legion* (1956), in which he shared billing with his young son Cuffy.

Since the TV series, he has kept acting to a minimum, making an occasional western. Now residing in New York, his time is spent as aquatic director of the Hotel Concord, on Lake Kiamesha in the Catskill mountains; supervising activities

From *Tarzan and his Mate* when the jungle togs were at their most abbreviated

of his swimming pool corporation; and operating his boys' camp in the Catskills.

MGM, ignoring Lesser's obviously inferior production, continued on their second Tarzan film and in mid-April, 1934, *Tarzan and his Mate*, the greatest of the Weissmuller series, was released.

The story by J. Kevin McGuiness, as adapted by Howard Emmett Rogers and Leon Gordon, began with Harry Holt (Neil Hamilton) returning to Africa with Marlin Arlington (Paul Cavanaugh) to secure the ivory fortune at the elephant burial

grounds. Their safari was first attacked by murderous natives, then by a tribe of gorillas which hurled boulders at them. Tarzan's cry stopped the apes and he and Jane led the remnants of the party to the burial grounds.

En route, Tarzan took time out to battle a rhinoceros (Weissmuller actually rode on the back of one for the scene) and a fourteen-foot crocodile that pursued the semi-nude Maureen O'Sullivan in some beautifully photographed underwater shots. At the climax, Tarzan charged with his elephant army to ward off the treacherous lion people, who killed the entire safari and nearly got Jane, too.

A charming scene in the middle of the picture showed the wounded and unconscious Tarzan treated by a band of concerned apes. The pantomime of the men in ape-suits diagnosing and treating his wound was novel in this film, but Metro's repeated use of this kind of gimmick turned their Tarzan pictures into corn in later years.

83

Crabbe and Edgar Rice Burroughs

Crabbe with Rick Vallin in Columbia's *King of the Congo* serial, 1951

*Tarzan and his Mate* was considered a rarity by *Time* Magazine, judging it "a sequel which is better than its original. . . . It is impossible to deny that the production is brilliant, the showmanship superb and the general effectiveness enormously impressive, even in moment when you suspect that the adventures are laid on just a trifle thickly."

When filming began at Lake Sherwood in Ventura County in late 1933, it was Rod LaRocque, famed silent screen matinee idol, who played Neil Hamilton's partner. And Cedric Gibbons, Metro's top art director who had always wanted to direct, was given *Tarzan and his Mate* to test his directing ability.

With over one-third of the picture completed, production halted. "A writing problem was the reason they gave," recalled Neil Hamilton, "and we didn't work for two weeks. When they called us back, Rod wasn't there. He had been replaced by Paul Cavanaugh. We never knew why." More than likely, his voice was considered unsuitable for the talkies and he went the way of John Gilbert. He had made only one talking picture prior to this assignment, but he made quite a few later in the forties.

Crabbe holds Miss Wells and holds off Edward Woods

Crabbe in Paramount's *King of the Jungle,* 1933, with Frances Dee

LaRocque having been replaced, the crew started from scratch. Then, nearly half-finished, filming was once again suspended, but only for a week. Upon resuming production, a new director, Jack Conway, replaced Gibbons, who had shot some 127,000 feet of useless film. Most of the cast hated to see "Gibby" go because he was easy to work with and Conway wasn't. Although Conway finished the picture and reshot a great deal, it is Gibbons who is given full credit for direction. Gibbons returned to art direction and designed most of the sets used in the Tarzan series.

More troubles awaited *Tarzan and his Mate* after its release. MGM had left themselves open for criticism for the scant wardrobe worn by Miss O'Sullivan. In one scene Tarzan tugs on Jane's garment and dives into the water. She follows, and when she surfaces a breast is exposed. Although done in good taste, the scene was later cut to please the Hays censorship office, which considered it too erotic. Miss O'Sullivan's lovely figure was never again shown off to such advantage. And Tarzan, too, had to abide by the new puritanism in films. His brief loincloth was lengthened into veritable leather shorts.

85

# ⑨ BURROUGHS-TARZAN ENTERPRISES

In the early thirties, Tarzan pictures were tremendous "box office" in the United States and consistently outgrossed all other pictures in the foreign market. In some Asian and West European countries, the Tarzan films would open in a black tie premiere. Haile Selassie, Emperor of Ethiopia, personally requested prints of Metro's Tarzan movies. About seventy-five percent of the Apeman's total gross came from foreign countries.

Motivated by all that jungle gold, three men came to Burroughs with a proposition one night in the summer of 1934. They were George W. Stout, Ben S. Cohen, and Ashton Dearholt, a silent screen actor who was acquainted with ERB. What they wanted was to form a film company with ERB as a fourth partner. Their chief business "would be to promote Burroughs' works." Thinking it a great idea, the Master threw in with them. This way he could share some of the huge profits the studios made in production and distribution. Although Lesser gave him an advance

and a promised participation in the profits, all Metro had given him was about $75,000, while they made several million on their first two Tarzan films. And since Metro had no Tarzan rights left, ERB had a free hand to produce his own pictures.

Their first project was to be a film based on an original story roughed out by ERB, called "Tarzan and the Green Goddess." As a full partner, ERB was paid no advance, but assured of an equal cut and allowed to select the actor to portray the Apeman. From over a hundred candidates, Burroughs chose Herman Brix, who had nearly had the lead in MGM's *Tarzan the Apeman.* Burroughs fondly cherished the hope that his hero would be presented as he created him.

Since they had no studios, they felt the picture should be filmed on location, somewhat closer than Africa. Ashton Dearholt, a rather swarthy adventurer, suggested Guatemala, and all agreed. With that setting in mind, Charles Royal and

Herman Brix in the Tarzan-like role of Kiroga in Republic's serial, *Hawk of the Wilderness*, 1938

Edwin Blum wrote a screenplay based on ERB's story and gave it the tentative working title of *Tarzan in Guatemala.*

In the late months of 1934, Dearholt led an expedition of twenty-nine cast and crew members, with tons of freight, via a huge liner, the *Seattle,* to the highland ruins of Guatemala. Under the direction of Edward Kull, aided by Wilber F. McGaugh, the picture, whose title was changed to *Tarzan and the Lost Goddess* then to *The New Adventures of Tarzan,* was finished in four months.

The story began with the Apeman leaving his estate in Africa to find his lost friend, D'Arnot, in Guatemala. En route, his aid was enlisted by Major Martling (Frank Baker) and his daughter, Alice (Dale Walsh), who were seeking hidden jewels in the Mayan ruins and a sacred idol containing the secret formula for a powerful explosive. In a lost city they discovered the idol and found D'Arnot imprisoned. They rescued both D'Arnot and the idol, only to have the statuette stolen by Raglan (Ashton Dearholt, who replaced the sick Don Castello), an explorer who had been trailing them. After Tarzan retrieved the idol, Ula Vale (Ula Holt), the mysterious heroine, revealed herself as Operator 17, a secret service agent representing the interests of the government. Jane did not appear in the picture and no gal was linked romantically with Tarzan.

Shortly before the company sailed for Central America, Dearholt's wife, Florence, filed divorce proceedings against her husband. Then while the expedition was in Guatemala, ERB, against the pleas of his family, divorced Emma Hulbert, his wife of thirty-four years. Four months later, on April 4, 1935, he married Florence Dearholt, who was thirty years younger. They went to Hawaii on an extended honeymoon and decided to stay there until things blew over.

Needing immediate cash and realizing that Burroughs-Tarzan Enterprises was not going to make it as a successful company for lack of adequate organization, ERB re-optioned Metro's contract, giving them a third Tarzan right. He also approved Lesser's sale of three of his remaining four film rights to MGM, who agreed to make a con-

88

Brix subdues Ashton Dearholt in BTE's *Tarzan and the Green Goddess*, 1938

From BTE's *New Adventures of Tarzan*, 1935. Brix, Merrill McCormick, Dale Walsh, and Louis Sargent

Ula Holt as a new Jane

Brix fights the lion

Brix with Frank Baker, Harry Ernest, and Ula Holt. Don Costello is in the background

siderable "authorization" payment to the author. Metro, extremely interested in following up their first two Tarzan films, had contacted ERB, who was in financial need. MGM then paid Lesser "a paltry $500,000" for these rights and also shelled out between $25,000 and $50,000 on each film to ERB.

Burroughs gained immediately from his deal with Metro, and lost relatively little in the long run by abandoning his own company, which was then preparing the *New Adventures of Tarzan* for release. In advance publicity for the picture they announced plans for other films based on ERB's books *The Mad King* and *Tarzan, Lord of the Jungle*, but these were never made. The complete output of the company amounted to four movies beyond its initial effort.

When *New Adventures* was released on June 21, 1935, Burroughs' partners found that MGM was campaigning heavily to keep their Tarzan picture

Brix as Tarzan in a dinner jacket

from getting good bookings. Metro managed to keep *New Adventures* out of nearly every big theatre in the country with their "block booking" policy: "Book *our* Tarzan later on or this one now."

Trying to make it as attractive to exhibitors as possible, *New Adventures* was offered in a variety of ways. Theatre managers could either rent it as a seven-reel seventy-five-minute feature complete, or as the seven-reel feature followed by eleven episodes, or as a twelve-chapter serial, the first couple of chapters being a resume of the feature. Their bookings, however, were limited to small independent chains.

Furthermore, trade reviews of this picture were unkind. *Variety* reported: "Limpid direction makes it fall way short of even the limited possibilities of an independent production. Herman Brix, who still gets billing as an Olympic champion, is at home in the Tarzan role, but even his robust endeavors fail to lift this production out of the mire of unimportant secondary dual spots." *Film Daily:* "Picture has enough hokum to make it acceptable for the small neighborhoods." The sincerity of these reviews is a bit doubtful in view of the fact that MGM had great influence on the trade papers. The opinion of the *Motion Picture Herald* is probably more trustworthy: "Spectacular and

Brix rescues Ula Vale and Dale Walsh

authentic, the picture having been made in Guatemala, {it} has a commercial worth that should not be ignored.''

MGM's boycott was effected because they felt the presentation of Tarzan as Burroughs created him would detract from their interpretation. Brix's portrayal was the only time between the silents and the 1960's that Tarzan was accurately depicted in films: he was mannered, cultured, soft-spoken, a well-educated English lord who spoke several languages, and didn't grunt. The deliberate attempt at authenticity in *New Adventures* is further evidenced in that the Apeman's chimp companion was called ''Nkima,'' as in the Tarzan novels, not ''Cheetah'' as Metro renamed him.

Since MGM had little control over the foreign market, *New Adventures* played important and lucrative engagements overseas. On the strength of the one picture alone, Brix became twentieth in popularity in France and Britain. And because of its fidelity to the books, the film has become a classic and was in almost continuous release throughout the world until its sale to television in 1961.

In fact, in June of 1938, Burroughs-Tarzan Enterprises edited a seventy-two minute feature film from the last ten chapters of the serial and re-

leased it under the title of *Tarzan and the Green Goddess*. With some previously unused footage added, the plot differs slightly, but basically the action is repeated. The billing was changed in 1940 to star Bruce Bennett, the name under which Brix became famous in films.

Following *New Adventures*, Brix made half a dozen serials for Republic, including a Tarzan-like role as Kioga in *Hawk of the Wilderness* (1938). Then after a few quickies for producer Sam Katzman, Herman Brix ceased to exist. Feeling the need for more training, Brix temporarily dropped out of films and enrolled in an acting workshop. He realized the necessity to avoid identification with Tarzan and his athlete background. After considerable deliberation, he changed his name to Bruce Bennett.

Soon thereafter, he was discovered by Warner Brothers in a play and offered a screen test. When the casting director, Steve Trilling, saw him, he exclaimed, ''You're Brix! You made that Tarzan film and those cheapies for Katzman.''

''I'm Bruce Bennett, now,'' Brix answered. ''What difference does it make? I proved I can act.''

''Well, we're not interested in your caliber of personnel here,'' Trilling replied, and the interview was closed.

Brix as a star shotputter in the 1928 Olympics

A few years later, after Bennett had made a name for himself at Paramount, Columbia, and Universal, Warners invited him back and, without reference to their previous encounter, gave him a featured player's contract. Bennett gained fame as a leading man in pictures like *Sahara, Atlantic Convoy, Task Force, Treasure of the Sierra Madre, Dark Passage, Strategic Air Command,* and many others.

In 1960, he retired from acting and went into the vending machine business. In seven years he rose from salesman to sales manager of Interstate United Corporation, which had become a multi-million dollar business. Although the money was big, he tired of the sixteen-hour days, and in February of 1967 he returned to acting, doing TV guest appearances.

Morris and Eleanor Holm.

Weissmuller and Miss O'Sullivan in *Tarzan Escapes*. Note how Jane's costume is lengthened and broadened.

Miss O'Sullivan and two lion cubs on the set of *Tarzan Escapes*.

# 10 TWO TARZANS TOO MANY

Just as *New Adventures of Tarzan* was being cut and edited, Metro put their first of four new Tarzan film rights into production. They were anxious to continue the flow of jungle gold into their studio treasury.

The first two in the MGM series, *Tarzan the Apeman* and *Tarzan and his Mate,* had been successful largely because no expense had been spared. Thalberg had insisted on doing them properly and production costs soared to over a million dollars each. The returns, in time, dwarfed expenses and justified Thalberg's policies. The third of this Weissmuller-O'Sullivan series, *Tarzan Escapes,* ran up a bill which equalled the previous two combined. And failing, for many reasons, to have the draw of the earlier films, *Tarzan Escapes* caused Metro to question their long-range plans for the series.

For this film, MGM constructed an extravagant tree-house for Tarzan and Jane. The set designers went way out to lend comfort and intimacy to this home that included everything from a baking oven of dried mud to a fan that was operated by Cheetah. The bed on which the Apeman whispered monosyllabic love to his mate was of bamboo and tropical leaves, surrounded on all sides by a myriad of luxurious furs. And admittance was gained by an elevator run on elephant power.

Cyril Hume, who had scripted *Apeman,* wrote a scenario titled *The Capture of Tarzan,* under the supervision of associate producer Sam Zimbalist, who has since produced many great films, such as the Academy Award winning *Ben Hur.* The story concerned a white hunter, Captain Fry (John Buckler), who tried to take Tarzan back to civilization in a cage to be displayed as a wild beast. He arrived in the jungle with Jane's cousins, Eric and Rita Parker (Bill Henry and Benita Hume, Cyril's daughter), who sought Jane's assistance in claiming a fortune that has been left to her. Fry's accomplice was a pudgy, nervous Englishman, Jiggs (Herbert Mundin), whose main

Weissmuller and Bill Henry in MGM's *Tarzan Escapes,*
1936.

purpose was to support the chimp in comic relief.

This screenplay, as directed by James McKay, made an exciting epic with many gruesome scenes. For instance, when the safari was captured by the bloodthirsty Ganelonis, the natives spread-eagled everyone to be butchered in a two-part ritual: a savage cutting with knives followed by a rock-swing to the head, cracking the skull open. Tarzan came on the scene to rescue the principals in a cliff-hanging sequence. Then, on the way of safety, the survivors crossed a swampy marsh-land thick with low-hanging fog, murderous pygmies, vampire bats and giant lizards. The prop department devised huge wired bats that descended suddenly upon the party and made off with screaming victims. And Tarzan, who had been earlier captured and then escaped, took a sadistic, yet fitting, revenge on Captain Fry in a lizard cave.

*The Capture of Tarzan* was finished in late 1935 and screened to preview audiences. The film terrified the children and brought outraged complaints from irate mothers and women's organizations. It is important to remember that the *Frankenstein* and *Dracula* films made in this era were considered "adult" films and not fit for children. In fact, two years later when Walt Disney released his wonderful *Snow White and the Seven Dwarfs,* narrow-minded, over-protective groups complained loudly that the cartoon witch was too horrible for children to watch.

Afraid that if released in its present form, *Capture* would be heavily criticized and alienate more people than it would attract, studio bosses ordered all gruesome scenes cut and replaced with re-takes. When director Jim McKay opposed the "retreat-and-please-everyone" tactics, he was replaced by John Farrow, who took the opportunity

Weissmuller and John Buckler.

to get to know Miss O'Sullivan better. They fell in love and were married in 1937. Of their seven children, only Mia (Mrs. Frank Sinatra) pursued an acting career.

The producer, still unhappy with results, pulled Farrow out and gave the film to Richard Thorpe, who directed the rest of the MGM series. After many months of hard work, director Thorpe achieved a complete reversal in overall effect, even retitling it *Tarzan Escapes*. The film was watered down "to appeal to young and old alike." The much-publicized vampire bat sequence was cut; instead, the crocodile fight from *Tarzan and his Mate* was re-used. The Ganelonis

Weissmuller with Bill Henry, Benita Hume, and Miss O'Sullivan.

became less ferocious, and the standard ending for MGM Tarzan films was reinstated, with the elephants breaking up the native village to rescue the safari. Also, more footage was interspersed of the chimp's overdone antics.

In essence, this film marked the third major step in lowering the Tarzan series to the child's level: the first being Sol Lesser's inferior and saccharine production of *Tarzan the Fearless;* immediately followed by the prudish Hays Office's morality ruling on Jane's realistic garb in *Tarzan and his Mate;* and now the jack-rabbit, sanguine compromise on what could have been a first-class adventure film.

The Tarzan series paid dearly for the compromise. Budget liabilities doubled; and since the series was making a lot of money, any expense that did not have justification on other films was chalked up against *Tarzan Escapes.* In shameless account juggling, even studio parties were marked off as Tarzan expenses.

Two years after production initially began, *Tarzan Escapes* opened at the Capitol Theatre in New York on November 16, 1936. *Variety* observed that "the tree-to-tree stuff has worn pretty thin for adult consumption. Appeal of the film will be mostly for children, and that's not likely to mean more than mediocre returns. While at first the sight of Tarzan doing everything but playing pinochle with his beast pals was a novelty, it's all pretty silly now. Derisive laughter greeted the picture too often. . . ."

Dribbling out into neighborhood theatres, the

film was received with mixed emotions. The *Philadelphia Exhibitor* recognized that "Metro spent time, money remaking *Tarzan Escapes,* but the result . . . is plenty of hokum." *Time* wrote: "Cinemaddicts with good memories of MGM's previous Tarzan pictures, though they may feel that they have seen *Tarzan Escapes* before, will find it richly entertaining." But Ed Connor, a staunch fan and critic, was disappointed: "It was a let-down after the action-packed *Tarzan and his Mate.*"

Sensing a weakness in the MGM series, Sol Lesser decided to exercise his remaining Tarzan film right. He assigned screenwriters Robert Lee Johnson and Jay Vann to work up a story and set about casting.

Since the last three screen Tarzans had been Olympic athletes, he began following sports closely. The 1936 Olympic decathlon champion, Glenn Morris, came to his attention in January, 1937, when Morris was awarded the Sullivan Award, which is given to the outstanding amateur athlete of the year. Morris, who had been a famed footballer at Colorado State College of Agriculture, won the Award over Jesse Owens, the triple Olympic champion Negro sprinter.

After casting the elated Morris as Tarzan, Lesser than contracted for Eleanor Holm Jarrett, champion backstroke swimmer, who had been dropped from the U.S. Olympic team for breaking training rules on the way to the 1936 Olympic games, to play the romantic lead. Johnson

and Vann rewrote their script of *Tarzan's Revenge* to employ Miss Holm's swimming ability. She more or less played herself in the film and was called Eleanor, even though she became the Apeman's mate at the conclusion. Lesser's explanation of this scripting was that, "being so well-known, Eleanor would not have been as acceptable to the general public as Jane."

*Tarzan's Revenge* was filmed by Lesser's Principal Productions on the back lots of Twentieth Century-Fox, and it was distributed by that company. D. Ross Lederman was director of this low-budget project. Its rather unconvincing plot had Eleanor and her millionaire parents (George Barbier and Hedda Hopper) hunting big game in

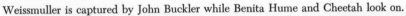

Weissmuller is captured by John Buckler while Benita Hume and Cheetah look on.

From *Tarzan Escapes.*

the jungle, accompanied by her sniveling fiancé (George Meeker). A swarthy, turbaned nabob called Ben Alleu Bey (C. Henry Gordon) marked Eleanor as an addition to his 100-wife harem. But Tarzan, who also took a fancy to her, stole her away for himself.

*Tarzan's Revenge* was Lesser's worst failure of the sixteen Tarzan films he eventually produced. He himself called it a "cheap quickie." "Morris was no actor," he said. *Time* didn't think so either: "This new Tarzan is lean, 6 ft. 2 in.

Glenn Morris, summoned to replace Johnny Weissmuller . . . {He} heroically combines the facial qualities of Broadway's Burgess Meredith and Hollywood's Harpo Marx, but has the acting ability of neither."

Released on January 7, 1938, *Tarzan's Revenge* lacked the gloss and spectacularity of the MGM films. The reviews reflected its dullness. *Film Daily* said "it suffers from repetition and a slow pace." *Variety:* "Even the youngsters, at which this type of production is aimed, will not be

The much-publicized devil bat sequence which was cut from the final version of *Tarzan Escapes.*

100

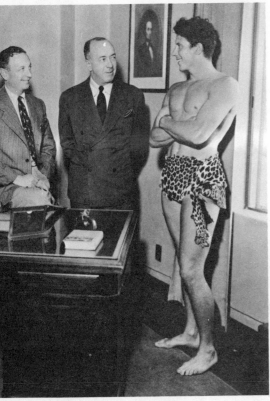

Producer Sol Lesser and Mr. Burroughs discuss with Glenn Morris the production plans for *Tarzan's Revenge*.

AN ORIGINAL M·G·M TARZAN HIT GREATEST OF ALL!

M·G·M PRESENTS

M-G-M'S ALL-TIME GREAT

TARZAN ESCAPES

WITH

*Johnny* WEISSMULLER
*Maureen* O'SULLIVAN

BASED UPON THE CHARACTERS CREATED BY
EDGAR RICE BURROUGHS
DIRECTED BY RICHARD THORPE
A METRO-GOLDWYN-MAYER PICTURE

AGAIN
TARZAN'S LOVE CALL RINGS
THROUGH THE JUNGLE!

Morris and Cheetah.

Morris with Eleanor Holm on the set
of *Tarzan's Revenge,* 1938.

Olympic decathlon star Glenn Morris
as the eighth film Tarzan.

Still from *Tarzan's Revenge.*

Morris and Cheetah.

much impressed." "It's greatest lack," wrote John Mosher in the *New York*, "is in the two leads. {Both} have many rows to hoe before they can be called actors . . . either good or bad." *Liberty* magazine went so far as to call Miss Holm "one of the year's worst actresses."

In addition to lowering the Tarzan films another notch, *Revenge* also caused considerable confusion as to who was really Tarzan. There was Weissmuller; but here were other pretenders to the loincloth—Morris and Herman Brix, who was making the rounds in the re-hash, *Tarzan and the Green Goddess*. Fortunately, Buster Crabbe, who was still remembered from his 1933 appearance, was really Flash Gordon and couldn't be Tarzan, but that still left two Tarzans too many.

At a Hollywood party, while *Tarzan's Revenge* was still in production, Morris was introduced as the new Tarzan. Lupe Velez, who was present without Weissmuller, ran up to Morris and kicked him in the shins. "You are not heem! There is onlee one Tarzan. And that's my Johnnee!" she cried.

The confusion arising from three Tarzans was dispelled when *Tarzan Finds a Son* was released

the following year. This picture affirmed Weissmuller's position as king of the cinema jungle until he chose to turn in his loincloth in 1948. With Lesser having produced his last film right, exclusive rights to the Tarzan character reverted to MGM as had been promised by their 1931 contract. Metro and Weissmuller had out-Tarzaned all the others.

Shortly after *Tarzan's Revenge* opened, Tarzan Morris sped back to his home town, Denver, Colorado, to escape the reviews. He then reappeared in Los Angeles and became a successful insurance agent. When Pearl Harbor was attacked, he enlisted in the Navy, earned the rank of an officer; was wounded in combat, and spent a great deal of time recovering in the Navy Hospital in San Francisco. He never made another film. Neither did Eleanor Holm, who resumed her swimming career in Billy Rose's "Aquacade."

The most famous Tarzan family.

# 11 THE TROUBLE WITH JANE

Although the studio kept Weissmuller idle between films, not allowing him to play other movie parts for fear they would damage his screen image, his co-star Maureen O'Sullivan was appearing in a great variety of roles. In fact, she made three pictures to every Tarzan film, unsuccessfully trying to avoid identification with Jane. The Tarzan pictures were usually scheduled around her other commitments and her seemingly continuous pregnancies. On several occasions, she worked right up to the eighth month, carrying large baskets of fruit to hide her condition.

Her three appearances as Jane since 1931 had typed her to a degree and she resented the limitations it placed on her career, as well as the continued ribbing of friends and fellow actors.

When producer Sam Zimbalist and director Richard Thorpe notified her that production would soon commence on the fourth in the Tarzan series, she raged that she had had enough of the jungle. In a meeting with screenwriter

Cyril Hume, they decided that they would try to give Miss O'Sullivan a reprieve from the series. "Not a reprieve," she pressured, "I want out permanently!"

What could be more permanent than death? So together they conspired to have Jane killed toward the end of the film, which they tentatively called *Tarzan in Exile*. In order to retain the family audience after Jane's death, Hume suggested they add a son. But since Tarzan and Jane weren't legally married, they'd have to adopt a child or be open to a new wave of criticism from the Legion of Decency.

Upon this groundwork, Hume wrote a screenplay about a young couple (Laraine Day and Morton Lowry) who were killed in a plane crash in the jungle. Their son was found by Tarzan and Jane, who named him Boy and raised him. Five years later, a search party (comprised of Ian Hunter, Henry Wilcoxen, Frieda Inescort and Henry Stephenson) came looking for the boy, who

107

Weissmuller in underwater action.

Weissmuller and Cyrus Kendall.

Weissmuller in *Tarzan's New York Adventure*, 1942.

Weissmuller, Miss O'Sullivan, and Johnny Sheffield in MGM's *Tarzan Finds a Son*, 1939.

was heir to several million dollars. After convincing Jane that the best thing for the boy was to return to civilization and get an education, she consented, against Tarzan's will, to lead them out of the jungle. They were captured by a hostile tribe and, in the same ritual concocted for *Capture of Tarzan* four years before, were almost put to death. In the predictable elephant-herd-to-the-rescue conclusion, Jane was mortally wounded and died.

Weissmuller personally chose five-year-old Johnny Sheffield for the role of Boy, which was inspired by Bobby Nelson's part in *Tarzan the Mighty* (1928). Sheffield was a husky kid with a

Tarzan throws the courtroom into a panic.

natural flair for athletics, quickly learning to swim under Johnny's watchful eyes. With his hair long, Johnny, Jr., looked like a miniature image of Weissmuller, almost as if he really were his son. Weissmuller looked after him, thinking this was the son he had wanted from Lupe.

*Tarzan in Exile* was shot entirely on location at Silver Springs, Florida, because the lakes there are the clearest in America, ideal for the extensive underwater photography.

During production, producer Zimbalist issued a routine release announcing Jane's forthcoming

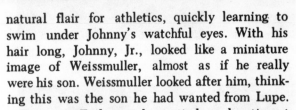

Weissmuller and Philip Dorn, Tom Conway, Miss O'Sullivan, and Johnny Sheffield in MGM's *Tarzan's Secret Treasure*, 1941.

Weissmuller with Reginald Owen, Tom Conway, Philip Dorn and Miss O'Sullivan.

A jungle wrestling match.

Tarzan rides a baby elephant.

death. Burroughs, who was in Hawaii at the time, paled when he read the news. He wired the studio, threatening to sue. But MGM regretfully informed ERB that the scenes with Tarzan and Boy at Jane's grave had already been shot and the crew was on its way home from Florida. They also reminded ERB that while their contract forbade them to kill, mutilate, or undermine the character of Tarzan, it didn't mention Jane. MGM was free to rub her out and Burroughs was powerless to stop them.

Howls of protest from the fans proved so loud, however, that the studio had to ressurect her. They rewrote the script, having Jane recover from the near-fatal wound in Tarzan's arms, saying that she had been wrong to disobey him. The film was retitled *Tarzan Finds a Son* and released June 16, 1939. And Miss O'Sullivan received a hike in salary.

*Variety*, which had panned the previous three Tarzans, had a change of heart: "*Tarzan Finds a Son* carries more credulity and believable jungle adventure than the long list of preceding Tarzan features during the past twenty years. Apeman's chumming attitude with wild beasts and previously elaborated tree-swinging have been minimized . . . it's under a handicap, though, due to absurdities and widly impossible situations that were spread pretty thick in the earlier Tarzan films."

B. R. Crisler of the *New York Times*, however,

From *Tarzan Finds a Son.*

Weissmuller with Henry Wilcoxen, Ian Hunter, Frieda Inescourt, and Johnny Sheffield.

felt like gently chiding Metro "for such monstrosities as a lion up a tree, apes riding elephants to the rescue. Also, you would think Tarzan's language might have improved a little after all these years of exposure to Jane's impeccable diction, but it hasn't. He still grunts like a Creek Indian, and articulates in a minimum of words, without conjunctions."

Choosing *Tarzan Finds a Son* as its "Movie of the Week," *Life* expressed the majority opinion that "by the addition of a young boy to the Tarzan family, the future of the series seems assured."

MGM, too, felt this way and gave Weissmuller a new seven-year contract, complete with studio-protective option intervals. Author Burroughs, however, vowed that Metro would acquire no rights in addition to the two they had left, one of which was already going through pre-production planning.

The next film, *Tarzan's Secret Treasure*, was produced by B. P. Fineman for Metro, with

Richard Thorpe directing. The exaggerated original screenplay by Myles Connolly and Paul Gangelin concerned a scientific expedition that inadvertently discovered that there was gold on Tarzan's lofty escarpment. The expedition, led by Professor Elliott (Reginald Owen), included good-humored O'Doul (Barry Fitzgerald) and villains Medford (Tim Conway) and Vandermeer (Philip Dorn), who kidnapped Jane and Boy in order to force Tarzan into revealing the whereabouts of the gold. All in turn (by Metro formula) were captured by natives; and Tarzan and elephants again charged to the rescue.

With the budget cutback suffered after the death of Irving Thalberg, some corners were cut in production. In the climax, many stock shots from *Tarzan Escapes* were used. And for the third time the crocodile fight from *Tarzan and his Mate* appeared.

Watching MGM production more closely since their abortive attempt to kill off Jane, ERB objected to a scene in which Tarzan threw back his head and laughed long and loud at the reaction of the treasure hunters to their first glimpse of the gold. Burroughs, who was not inclined to laugh at money, demanded the sequence be deleted. Tarzan, he said, was reserved, and boisterous laughter was strictly out of character. The scene was taken out.

Released in December, 1941, *Tarzan's Secret Treasure* boasted of having been in production two years. The *Hollywood Reporter* was closer to the truth: "MGM wisely allows sufficient time to elapse between Tarzan pictures so public appetite is whetted for the continuation of the ever-popular series . . . Certainly no one can take the events of this yarn seriously." And *Variety* applauded Thorpe's direction: "He lards the swift action with plenty of laughs and generally treats the material in a pseudo-serious manner for top-notch results."

By this time, the whimsical approach to the Tarzan series earmarked it as purely kid stuff. Weissmuller, who loved kids and now had a son by his third wife, Beryl Scott, was satisfied to do it just for children. Maureen O'Sullivan, who still wanted out of the series, was even less happy with the gradual slipping away of the dignity connected with the early films. It was somewhat of a comfort to her that Metro's policy of using

name actors in supporting roles continued to the end.

In *Tarzan's New York Adventure*, the last of the MGM series, producer Frederick Stephani tried to appease Miss O'Sullivan by giving her a contemporary setting and a fashionable wardrobe to wear. Myles Connolly and William Lipman wrote an imaginative screenplay called *Tarzan Against the World*, based on Connolly's original story.

The action had Tarzan and Jane following a circus owner, Buck Rand (Charles Bickford), who kidnapped Boy to perform in his show. Rand was accompanied by animal trainer Mountford (Chill Wills) and Jimmie Shields (Paul Kelly) who flew them out of the jungle against his will. Tarzan, Jane and Cheetah followed them to New York, where a certain amount of humor was natural in the Apeman's struggle to put on a double-breasted suit and in his reactions to gadgets like telephones and radios. For the first time in sound films, Tarzan wore clothes. A classic comment from him at his first glimpse of New York from a plane: "Stone jungle."

In the big city, at a trial for the boy's custody, Tarzan was provoked into violence and jailed. He escaped, and when police pursued, he dived off the Brooklyn Bridge into the East River. For the scene, a look-alike dummy was tossed from the bridge. Finally, locating the circus with the help of the pilot's girl friend (Virginia Grey), Tarzan enlisted the captive elephants to wreck the circus and rescue Boy, repeating the Metro-pattern conclusion a final time.

Weissmuller and Miss O'Sullivan reading the Tarzan comic strip between scenes of *Tarzan's Secret Treasure*.

Weissmuller and director Richard Thorpe discuss *Tarzan's New York Adventure*.

Looking over a miniature model of headhunters' village in *Tarzan Finds a Son*.

Weissmuller personally selected Johnny Sheffield for the role of Boy.

On the assumption that movie-goers' memories are short, *Tarzan Against the World* began with the oft-used crocodile fight. A week prior to its release, on April 15, 1942, the title which seemed to promise too much, was changed by the producer to *Tarzan's New York Adventure*.

The film, although superior to *Tarzan's Secret Treasure*, was not received as well. The sight of Tarzan in tailored suits was too much for the hard-core fans. Although *New York Adventure* wasn't a financial boon, the *Hollywood Reporter* nailed it as "the most adult of the Tarzan series."

With this picture, MGM ended its association with Tarzan. World War II had cost the studios a good chunk of their lucrative foreign markets, which meant at least fifty percent of the Apeman's grosses. And having exhausted all their Tarzan film rights, MGM failed to pick up Weissmuller's option, which had come up again for renewal.

Sol Lesser, who had been a spectator eager for active participation since 1938, made a bid for Weissmuller's contract and took him to RKO for more of the same. And Johnny Sheffield, too. But the invitation Lesser extended to Maureen O'Sullivan to join them was flatly refused. Pleased to be free of the role, the prettiest of Tarzan's Janes went on to complete over eighty dramatic films, and eventually made her debut on Broadway in *Never Too Late*. In recent years, she has been a regular on NBC-TV's *Today* Show, *Alcoa Presents* and *Playhouse 90*.

The dive from the Acapulco cliffs which killed Angel
Garcia, Weissmuller's double during filming of RKO's
*Tarzan and the Mermaids*, 1948.

Weissmuller trains an elephant in *Tarzan and the Huntress.*

# 12 THE APEMAN GROWS FAT WITH DISCONTENT

Miss O'Sullivan's departure from the series forced Lesser to omit Jane from his first two Tarzan films at RKO. In the first, *Tarzan Triumphs,* her absence is explained in a letter which states she is visiting relatives in England; in the second, *Tarzan's Desert Mystery,* another letter tells of her nursing British soldiers.

During the early stages of production on *Tarzan Triumphs,* producer Lesser was contacted by the State Department, which considered Tarzan an important propaganda weapon. They were most eager to have films show that democracy will be victor only if it is alive and active, not complacently inert in its corner of the world. A great believer in freedom, Lesser agreed to do what he could.

Upon this theme, Carroll Young wrote an original story in which he tried to make Tarzan a symbol of freedom and the spokesman for the American idea. He and Roy Chansler adapted the screenplay, which began with Zandra (Frances Gifford), white princess of a lost civilization, coming to Tarzan for help. The Nazis (under command of Stanley Ridges, Rex Williams, Sig Ruman, and Phillip Van Zandt) had invaded the jungle intent on conquering her peaceful people in order to take possession of their wealth in tin and oil.

At first Tarzan, playing the supreme isolationist and uninterested in helping her enslaved people, merely said, "Nazi go away." To which Zandra replied, "You don't know them. Once they conquer us, they will spoil everything you stand for." When the Nazis took a few pot shots at him and captured Boy (Sheffield), Tarzan got the message and came across with this line: "Now Tarzan make war!" At this point, audiences literally got to their feet and cheered. Tarzan's commando tactics brought the film to a thrilling finish.

Released in January, 1943, thirteen months after the United States entered World War II, *Tarzan*

115

Weissmuller with Acquanetta in RKO's *Tarzan and the Leopard Woman*, 1946.

*Triumphs* was Lesser's biggest earner, realizing ERB, Incorporated, more than a quarter of a million dollars. Credit for the film's success goes to Lesser for the new vitality he instilled in the series by setting it in contemporary times. His casting of beautiful Frances Gifford was also a strong plus. Earlier at Republic Studios she had played Nyoka, the ERB-created female version of Tarzan, in *Jungle Girl*.

Reviewers compared Lesser's production with Metro's. *Variety* reported: "First of the Sol Lesser Tarzan pictures with Johnny Weissmuller . . . does not stack up against initial two or three Metro-produced, but tops later films in series . . . (a) graphic illustration of what careful production-helming can do with a budgeted picture." *Film Daily* liked the fact that "More action than usual distinguishes the latter part of the film." And according to the *Hollywood Reporter*, "The script and its excellent direction by William Thiele mixes enough plausible incident to balance the

Johnny Sheffield as Bomba the jungle boy in Allied Artist's *Safari Drums*, 1953.

116

Weissmuller with Patricia Morrison and Sheffield in RKO's
*Tarzan and the Huntress,* 1947.

Weissmuller with Barton MacLane, Joan Warburton,
Charles Trowbridge, Patricia Morrison, and Brenda Joyce.

Brenda Joyce as Jane in *Tarzan and the Leopard Woman.*

more extravagant flights of pure fancy . . . Weissmuller's work is marked with practiced vigor."

Following completion of *Tarzan Triumphs,*
Johnny did a cameo walk-on as Tarzan in *Stage
Door Canteen,* a United Artists release which was
produced by Sol Lesser in association with the
American Theatre wing. It was a romantic hodge-
podge dealing with a soldier and a canteen hos-
tess, carried entirely by brief guest appearances
of stage and screen greats.

Lesser, a man prone to formula-grinding,
thought the government-inspired Tarzan propaganda film successful enough to merit a sequel.
The Apeman again came to grips with the Nazis
in a second picture called *Tarzan Against the
Sahara,* for which the screenplay was supplied
by Edward T. Lowe from a story by Carroll
Young. Kurt Newmann acted as associate producer for Lesser; Sheffield and Weissmuller continued in their roles.

The story was motivated by a letter from Jane
in England, asking Tarzan to send her a malaria
serum extracted from certain jungle plants. In his
search for these plants, Tarzan crossed a desert,
where he incurred the wrath of a German agent
(Otto Kruger) by spoiling his capture of a wild
horse. Arriving in an Arab city with Boy, he met
Connie Bryce (Nancy Kelly) a stranded American
lady magician, who, because of a secret message
she carried to the Sheik (Lloyd Corrigan), was
framed and sentenced to be hanged. When the
Apeman rescued her, they were marked for death
by Nazis agents.

Almost another picture starts in the final reels
when Tarzan must fight off prehistoric monsters
to obtain the fever cure. Advertising for the picture urged the public to "See! Tarzan fighting
prehistoric dinosaurs!" What actually developed
was Weissmuller superimposed on footage from
an old film like *One Million B.C.* He did, however, struggle with a man-eating plant and do
away with Nazis Kruger and his henchman (Joe
Sawyer) by throwing them to a giant spider. The
sequence with the spider was intended seriously,
but came across as amusing as the chimp's
comedy.

The picture remained uneven even though Les-
ser ordered most of the original version re-shot as
*Tarzan and the Sheik,* and then retitled *Tarzan's
Desert Mystery.* And although the last few reels

117

Weissmuller with J. M. Kerrigan, Don Douglas, Barton MacLane, and Henry Stephenson in RKO's *Tarzan and the Amazons,* 1945.

somewhat compensated for the laborious first half, as a whole the film was ragged, a product of the haste that pushed RKO to take quick advantage of the situation created by *Tarzan Triumphs.* One major fault was that too much attention was directed to Nancy Kelly, resulting in less footage of Weissmuller. The picture suffered accordingly.

*Tarzan's Desert Mystery* was released on December 8, 1943, just ten months after *Tarzan Triumphs.* Not since *Romance of Tarzan* was distributed on the tails of *Tarzan of the Apes* in 1918 had a film in the series followed another so closely. "Consequently," wrote the *Hollywood Reporter,* "*Desert Mystery* is in the bag right now as a film attraction. But it also must be

recorded that the entertainment falls below standard for the perennial series. It makes too many compromises and wanders too far from the domain where Tarzan is seen to best advantage." *Variety,* too, felt that the picture was "none too adroitly handled."

In an effort to boost the series, Lesser brought Jane back with the next film, *Tarzan and the Amazons.* She was played by Brenda Joyce, a tall, attractive blonde. "I don't know what the kids are going to think when they see me with a blonde Jane," Weissmuller had smiled. "Kind of looks like Tarzan's been playing the jungle a bit."

Kurt Neumann continued as associate producer on *Amazons* and also replaced Thiele as director due to the unfortunate results of the last film.

The Amazons look on as Weissmuller holds Shirley O'Hara in his arms.

Weissmuller with Miss O'Hara and Maria Ouspenskaya.

The screenplay by John Jacoby and Marjorie L. Pfaelzer had Tarzan protecting a hidden valley of women whose queen was played by Maria Ouspenskaya. A party of archaeologists (among which were Don Douglas, Henry Stephenson, and villain Barton MacLane) asked Tarzan to lead them to this undiscovered city of antiquity, but he refused. However, Boy, who also knew the way, was duped into guiding them there.

Unimpressed, *Variety* wrote about *Tarzan and the Amazons* on its release date, March 19, 1945: "Neumann, after a slow start, kept his action moving and made the characters as believable as the series allows."

After the completion of *Amazons*, Lesser granted Weissmuller's request for a leave of ab-

sence between pictures to pursue some straight dramatic roles. Johnny wanted to do some real acting in some films for Pine-Thomas Productions, a Paramount Studio unit that had offered him a non-exclusive contract for three pictures.

Johnny's passion for a straight part can best be illustrated by a story he was especially fond of telling: "I remember once (as Tarzan) I was supposed to point somewhere and say, 'You go.' I must've felt talkative that day because I pointed and said, 'You go quick.' 'Cut!' the director yelled. 'What's the matter, Johnny? We don't want to load this scene with any long speeches. Just do it like it's written.'"

The three-picture deal with Pine-Thomas was to become operative when and if they found the

Weissmuller with Otto Kruger in RKO's *Tarzan's Desert Mystery*, 1943.

Weissmuller with Joe Sawyer, Johnny Sheffield, and Nancy Kelly.

Weissmuller with Nancy Kelly, Johnny Sheffield, and Lloyd Corrigan.

Weissmuller with Frances Gifford and Johnny Sheffield in RKO's *Tarzan Triumphs*, 1949.

right properties for Weissmuller, two of which were to be war films, followed by a western. After several months of deliberation, plans for the war pictures were dropped because it was felt that the war would soon end and that particular market would be eliminated. Many screenplays for the western were considered, but all were rejected.

All too soon the time had run out; Lesser called him for the next Tarzan film. Weissmuller, who had slowly been gaining weight and grumbling recently about wanting a percentage of the gross receipts, was frustrated in the attempt to alter his image. In resignation, he lost about thirty pounds and went back to climbing trees.

The next in the series, *Tarzan and the Leopard Woman*, showed some improvement in Neumann's direction, which worked the situations in Carroll Young's original screenplay to full advantage. The introduction of a female menace, Lea (Acquanetta) high priestess of the leopard cult, was all to the good. Reminiscent of Queen La of Opar, she seemed an extension of actual Burroughsiana.

Sheffield and Joyce continued as Tarzan's family in the tightly plotted yarn about an African tribe who donned the skins and claws of the animal they worship and fanatically tried to retard the advance of civilization in the jungle. Tarzan picked up their trail when a jungle caravan was attacked. And when the leopard cult struck at Jane and Boy, he actively pursued their extermination, only to be captured by the native doctor (Edgar Barrier) and Anthony Caruso. Boy in the meantime was menaced by the Leopard Woman's younger brother (Tommy Cook).

In the old Metro days, Tarzan's predicament of being prepared for sacrifice to the leopard god would have been solved by throwing back his head and heralding his trusty elephant herd to the rescue. Lesser, however, was more inclined to use Cheetah as the saving grace. The chimp was always employed for comedy business as well as to be direct agent in many of the key situations. The way the chimp was so continuously depended upon to get the troops out of a tight scrape became an obsession with Lesser.

Tarzan and Boy in *Tarzan Triumphs.*

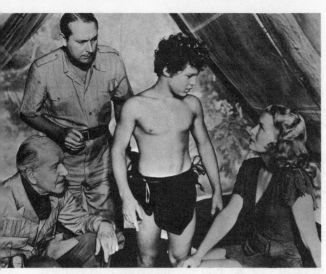

Brenda Joyce as Jane is shown here with Henry Stephenson, Don Douglas, and Johnny Sheffield in *Tarzan and the Amazons*.

Weissmuller with Brenda Joyce and Johnny Sheffield. This was Sheffield's last appearance as Boy. He outgrew the part.

Weissmuller in action.

The more extensive use of Cheetah as a pivotal character in plots was dangerous because, by nature, chimps are ferocious and unpredictable. They grow rapidly, and the older they are the more vicious and ill-tempered they become. Their long arms are strong enough to easily break a man's limb; and they itch to bite anyone who happens to strike them unfavorably.

Animal trainers usually worked with several look-alikes, never keeping the apes professional for more than five or six years. By that time they were too difficult to handle. During Johnny's picture career, he worked with some eight different chimps.

When he met Cheetah I back in 1931, the chimp bared his teeth, his sly eyes searching for a sign of weakness or fear. Drawing his hunting knife, Johnny held it close to Cheetah's nose so he recognized the object, then knocked it hard against the chimp's skull. After replacing the knife in its sheath, he offered Cheetah his hand. Momentarily, Cheetah glared at him in anger, then the inscrutable grin returned and he took Johnny's hand. From that instant there was a lasting friendship between them.

Weissmuller was never injured by any of the animals during his sixteen-year reign as Tarzan. He would always build a camaraderie with the animals before production and let them know that he was not afraid, nor would he take any nonsense from them. His method worked with all the animals except the near-sighted rhinoceros, Mary, that he rode in *Tarzan and his Mate* and the different crocodiles they used who would have as soon made a meal of him as race him in the water.

Disregarding the chimp's role in *Leopard Woman*, the film was a new triumph for Lesser. Said *Variety* about the February 8, 1946, release: "There isn't a dull moment in it." And Jack D. Grant in the *Hollywood Reporter* called *Leopard Woman* "one of the best adventures of the jungle man. . . ."

Continuing talks with Pine-Thomas Productions during production of *Leopard Woman* resulted in the selection of *Swamp Fire* as Weissmuller's first non-Tarzan starring vehicle. They paid him a record salary of $75,000 and said that any future films would be based on *Swamp Fire's* returns, which were to indicate Johnny's drawing power sans loincloth.

Supporting Weissmuller in the picture was pal Buster Crabbe, his swimming and jungle rival of a dozen years before. Weak in storyline, dialogue and direction, *Swamp Fire* did not set any attendance records. It was a mediocre adventure film and received little attention. Consequently, very few people are aware that Johnny ever made the film.

Immediate prospect of future projects for Pine-Thomas looked poor and Johnny cinched on his loincloth again. Why break the mold? he asked himself. He was lucky to be playing Tarzan. It was work that he liked and, after all, it was the Apeman that set him up, made an international figure of him, far beyond his swimming fame. Why not relax and enjoy it? He *was* fortunate. He decided that he would continue in the role until he was too old to swing on vines.

With new vigor he dieted and reported for *Tarzan and the Huntress* looking slimmer and more fit than he had in years. Released in March of 1947, the film was once again piloted by Kurt Neumann as associate producer and director.

Filmed at RKO Studios, like all the previous Lesser-Weissmuller pictures, *Tarzan and the Huntress* was from the original story and screenplay by Jerry Gruskin and Rowland Leigh. The plot revolved around a band of hunters supervised by a pretty animal trainer, Tanya (Patricia Morrison). With her were an unscrupulous financier (John Warburton) and a brutal trail boss (Barton MacLane). The shortages of zoo animals following World War II brought them to the jungle and, after negotiations with native King Farrod (Charles Trowbridge), they proceeded to trap more animals than the agreed upon quota. The Apeman then intervened on behalf of his four-legged friends. The climax was the familiar elephant stampede.

The storyline permitted the use of considerably more animal footage than had appeared in the last half-dozen films combined, providing the film with a solid selling point. *Variety* considered *Huntress* "one of the strongest of the Sol Lesser series. Film carries more movement and sincerity than majority in series and boasts largest number of wild beasts and animal sequences to date, adding up to top entertainment." "This is the type . . . preferred by the Tarzan following," added *Film Daily*.

The tremendous grosses earned by *Tarzan and*

Johnny Weissmuller in his twelfth year as the ape man.

the Huntress increased Johnny's discontentment with the $50,000 per picture he was drawing from Lesser. Even though he worked only about twelve weeks a year for that, he felt that he should be claiming a cut of the overall receipts, too. He mentioned it again to Lesser, who told him that they would work something out after his present contract, which had one film left on it, expired.

As it turned out, this next film, *Tarzan and the Mermaids,* was Weissmuller's final appearance as the Jungle Lord. It was also significant in several other ways. This was the first time Lesser had actually gone on location for a Tarzan film; it was filmed entirely in Mexico—in Acapulco and in studios at Churubusco and Mexico City. And, for the first time since 1939, Johnny Sheffield did not appear as Boy. Sheffield had become almost as large as Weissmuller, and according to Lesser, "he had outgrown the part." In *Mermaids,* he was said to be away at school in England. When Monogram Studios learned that he had been dropped from the series, they grabbed him for their *Bomba, the Jungle Boy* films, which were based on the novels by Roy Rockwood, obviously inspired by Tarzan.

Another first in *Mermaids* was the extensive use of music and singing, composed and conducted by Dimitri Tiomkin. The picture also featured a return to water and swimming sequences, including a fight with an octopus and cliff diving. During the filming of one diving sequence off the high Acapulco cliffs, Angel Garcia, doubling for Johnny, was killed after completing a spectacular dive, when a wave dashed him against the rocks. The incident shook Johnny badly.

*Mermaids* was written by Carroll Young, who had been responsible for the best treatments in the Lesser series. The story had Tarzan find Mara (Linda Christian), a young native girl who had run away from her native island because the high priest (George Zucco) was trying to force her to marry a villainous pearl trader (Fernandon Wagner), posing as the god Balu. Mara was recaptured by the natives and taken back to the island. But Tarzan and Jane (Brenda Joyce) rescued her and reunited her with her true fiance' (Gustavo Rojo), after exposing the false god.

Frances Gifford substituting for Jane in *Tarzan Triumphs.*

124

Even with all the things going for it and the competent direction of Robert Florey, *Tarzan and the Mermaids* was blandly average film-fare. "A great deal of time is wasted," judged the *Motion Picture Review,* with unnecessary detail and some deplorable singing, but Tarzan does all that one has come to expect of him."

When negotiations for future pictures came up, Weissmuller pressed for a percentage of the gross. Lesser, unwilling to concede, let Johnny go. After seventeen years and a dozen films, the most popular screen Tarzan laid down his loincloth for good.

Lesser told the press that by "mutual agreement, Weissmuller has made his last Tarzan film. No longer trim, he is too out of shape for the role." A man still impressed by Weissmuller's physique and his following was Sam Katzman, a producer at Columbia Studios with a reputation for making profitable low-budget pictures. He offered Johnny a percentage of the gross to do the lead in *Jungle Jim,* a film based on Alex Raymond's comic strip. "If it sells," he told Johnny, "we'll do a series." It did sell, and they did do, a series.

Between 1948 and 1956, Johnny appeared in twenty Jungle Jim films, which were almost as

Weissmuller between Linda Christian and George Zucco.

popular with fans as his Tarzans. Plots were way out—he tangled with pygmy moon men, a half-human killer ape, leopard woman, a tribe of million-year-old man-monsters and other fantastic creatures.

In essence, Johnny was still playing Tarzan, but fully-clothed. He even had a chimp companion, Tamba; later on it was an ape named Kimba.

His Jungle Jim series spawned a TV show in 1956, which after a two-year run went into syndication all over the world. On the average, Johnny's cut from the film and the TV series brought him $200,000 annually. His holdout for a percentage paid off.

When the Jungle Jim TV program expired, so did Weissmuller's acting career. His twenty-six years in the cinema jungles had mercilessly typecast him. Casting directors wouldn't even talk to

him about a part. After kicking around Hollywood for awhile, Johnny went into a forced retirement from the entertainment industry.

For the past ten years, he has been involved in sales and public relations for the General Swimming Pool Corporation in Chicago. With his fifth wife, Maria Bauman, he currently lives in Fort Lauderdale, Florida, where he is curator of the Swimming Hall of Fame. Although sixty-four years old, he still swims every day, plays golf frequently, and looks about fifteen years younger than he is.

His last appearance before the cameras was for a car commercial early this year. He yearns to be active in films again, even if he never discards the Tarzan image. "I don't mind if they keep pointing at me and saying, 'Hey, him Tarzan!'" says Weissmuller. "I love it!"

125

Lex Barker, the tenth Tarzan.

# 13 SOCIETY COMES TO THE JUNGLE

After negotiations with Johnny Weissmuller broke down, Sol Lesser assigned RKO director Lee Sholem the task of selecting the tenth Tarzan. Sholem swore that in the following months he "interviewed over a thousand actors and athletes, but not one was worthy of the loincloth abandoned by Weissmuller."

The search ended when Alexander (Lex) Crichlow Barker, an RKO contract player, went to Sholem's office to inquire about the part. "Well, where have you been hiding?" exclaimed the director, surveying Barker's six-foot-four, 203-pound, handsomely dignified physique. "If you want the job it's yours," concluded Sholem, as he reached for the phone to notify Lesser of his find.

Born May 8, 1919, of English-Spanish heritage, Lex Barker was a direct descendant of Roger Williams, founder of Providence, Rhode Island, and of Sir William Henry Crichlow, historical

governor-general of Barbados. With this distinguished family tree, Lex rated membership in the New York Social Register.

While attending Essenden prep school and Phillips-Exeter in New England, Barker excelled in football and track. After graduation from Exeter, he checked into Princeton University, but decided to be an actor instead and went into summer stock. A year later, a talent scout from 20th Century-Fox spotted him and arranged a screen test, which resulted in a contract offer. Before anything came of it, World War II started. He enlisted in the U.S. Infantry as a buck private and rose to the rank of major.

Following his discharge (because of a serious wound), he contacted Fox and was signed for a year, during which time he had only a bit role in *Dollface*. Accepting a new contract from Warner Brothers, he sat idle on the studio payroll again except for a couple of inconsequential roles. The

Barker with Dorothy Hart, his fourth Jane, in RKO's *Tarzan's Savage Fury*, 1952.

From RKO's *Tarzan's Peril*, 1951.

Barker and his Cheetah.

Joyce MacKenzie, Barker, Henry Brandon, and Lillian Molieri in RKO's *Tarzan and the She-Devil*, 1953.

128

Barker with Robert Bice and Raymond
Burr.

Barker with Robert Bice (holding rifle) and Monique
Van Vooren.

trouble seemed to be that he was too tall to play supporting parts to leading men and was too unknown to be a leading man himself.

Lex finally graduated to a leading man in *Tarzan's Magic Fountain,* which was released on January 13, 1949. Having idolized the character as a kid, he was thrilled. "If my muscles hold up and my waistline keeps down, I can play Tarzan till I'm fifty," said Lex in his initial enthusiasm. "Tarzan is progressing," he pointed out. "I have more dialogue than my predecessors. Two-syllable words, too. No more of the 'You Jane—me happy' stuff."

When Lex learned that the original screen Tarzan, Elmo Lincoln, had a bit part in *Magic Fountain,* he felt like a kid again. Lesser had hired Lincoln, realizing the tremendous publicity potential of having the first Tarzan appear in the premiere film of the tenth Tarzan. When Elmo sat in on one of Barker's interviews, he dominated it completely, complaining that the Tarzans since sound were completely different from the silents.

The screenplay by Curt Siodmak and Harry Chandlee was filmed under the title of *Tarzan and the Arrow of Death,* but was released as *Tarzan's Magic Fountain.* In the film, the Apeman tried to keep unscrupulous hunters (Albert Dekker and Charles Drake) from a hidden valley where there was a fountain of youth. They became aware of the fountain when a missing aviatrix (Evelyn Ankers) emerged from the jungle as young as she was when her plane went down many years before; she reverted to her real age after the effects of the magic fountain wore off.

"The story could lay claim to more concrete dramatic substance," wrote the *Hollywood Reporter,* "but its shortcomings are amply compensated for in production backgrounds and the expensive footage allotted to the animals. As for Barker's Tarzan, it is equal to any within memory of this reviewer and we're afraid that goes back to Elmo Lincoln. Barker's handsome physique fits the Burroughs description, and he is actor enough to make the jungle man a more animated person than he has been."

Brenda Joyce gave her fifth and final performance as Jane in *Magic Fountain.* Although her characterization was excellent, she wanted more time to spend with her children. Miss Joyce was the only actress besides Maureen O'Sullivan to become identified with the role of Jane. In the rest of his Tarzan series, producer Lesser recast

Barker with Charles Korbin.

Barker with Brenda Joyce and Cheetah.

Jane every picture, trying to find an actress with that elusive quality possessed by Maureen O'Sullivan and Brenda Joyce.

The next Jane was Vanessa Brown; the picture, *Tarzan and the Slave Girl*. Hans Jacoby and Arnold Belgard supplied the script in which Tarzan's job was to rescue Jane and Lola (Denise Darcel), a nurse, who were kidnapped and entombed by the Lionians. The ruler of the lost tribe (Hurd Hatfield) and his wicked advisor (Anthony Caruso) wanted the girls to help repopulate their civilization, which was dying from a strange disease. Thrills included fighting off a sinister native band called the Waddies, who disguised themselves as bushes and ambushed the Apeman's party with blow-guns.

As a half-breed nurse with a yen for men and an immediate fancy for Tarzan, Denise Darcel added a lot of spice to the film, especially when attired in a revealing sarong. Pictures of her hold-

ing on to Barker's leg appeared in many girlie magazines.

*Tarzan and the Slave Girl*, which was directed by Lee Sholem, premiered on March 15, 1950. Although *Variety* thought the film "neat adventuring" and "up to the general standard," *Photoplay* called it "too fantastic!" The *Film Reviewer* said: "Preposterous . . . has some unintentional laughs."

Although almost all of Tarzan's adventures were laid in Africa, none of the series had ever actually been filmed there. And Lesser, a small energetic man dedicated to the jungle hero, fancied going on location to give the next Tarzan film greater authenticity, and new energy, too, he thought, by shooting it in color. While the trip produced many miles of good background film, it proved a comedy of errors.

Through bad timing, the company, under direction of Phil Brandon, arrived in Africa in July

131

(1950), the middle of the winter below the equator. Moreover, the location site at the base of Mount Kenya was always so cloudy that Tarzan lost his tan, and an urgent call was sent to Hollywood for more body make-up. The chimps that had been brought along froze up and refused to cooperate. And since no chimpanzee with sufficient personality and acting ability could be found in Kenya, Cheetah had to be cut from Sam Newman and Francis Swann's screenplay, called *Tarzan and the Jungle Goddess*.

There were other troubles, according to Tarzan Barker: "We just weren't prepared for location conditions. Local natives were rounded up, and the first time I appeared in the jungle in my loincloth, they burst out laughing. It was demoralizing. Then the director wanted me to tangle with a man-eating plant. I told him that I would only wrestle a plant that had sense enough to let go on cue. I eventually battled one back in Hollywood that the RKO special effects department built."

With the bad weather getting worse and half the color film ruined in an accident, the troops made their way back to the States in late August. The director quit and Lesser summoned Byron Haskin to replace him. Haskin had the screenwriters rework and tighten the plot, which involved three escaped convicts (George Macready, Douglas Fowley, and Glenn Anders), who were supplying guns to a warlike native tribe headed by Fred O'Neal.

Retitled *Tarzan's Peril*, although released in Great Britain as *Tarzan and the Jungle Goddess*, the film briefly featured Virginia Huston as Jane dressed unusually in white animal skins. Dorothy Dandridge as Melnendi, the native queen, was particularly outstanding; she became famous later as a musical-comedy star on Broadway, TV, and in pictures like *Carmen Jones* and *Porgy and Bess*.

*Tarzan's Peril* opened in March, 1951, and was embraced by *Variety* as "exciting and suspenseful. . . . Expert editing and matching of backgrounds give the picture the semblance of having been lensed entirely in Africa."

The plans to make *Peril* the first Tarzan feature in color were discarded when a large portion of the color footage was spoiled on location. At that point, the film was converted to black and white. Some of those Technicolor background sequences, however, did turn up in later Tarzan pictures

after Lesser began using color in 1957.

Barker's fourth film, *Tarzan's Savage Fury*, was directed by Cyril Enfield and produced under the title of *Tarzan the Hunted*. For the film, which was released on March 18, 1952, Barker sported a beard and mustache. Dressing as a white hunter, he posed for a snapshot that was supposed to be of Tarzan's father, Lord Greystoke.

The story had to do with Tarzan's cousin, who came to the jungle in search of the Apeman to help secure a diamond fortune that was vital to England's military safety. The cousin was killed in the opening sequences by his guide, Rokov, a Russian agent (Charles Korvin), who persuaded an English traitor, Edwards (Patric Knowles), to impersonate Tarzan's cousin, offering Lord Greystoke's diary as proof of identification. The snapshot of Barker as Tarzan's father appeared in the diary and flashed on the screen for a brief second.

This film represented Lesser's first attempt to rebuild Tarzan's screen family. To develop the domestic portions of the screenplay, Lesser contacted Cyril Hume who had written *Tarzan Finds a Son* in 1938. Collaborating with Hume were Hans Jacoby and Shirley White. Not wanting to assault the memory of Johnny Sheffield's characterization of Boy, Lesser asked that they establish a new character that would perform the same function. They created Joey, a jungle waif rescued by Tarzan from natives who were using the boy as bait while hunting crocodiles.

Tommy Carlton was introduced as Joey, and Dorothy Hart appeared as Jane. For all purposes, Carlton merely recreated the role vacated by Johnny Sheffield in 1947. The *Hollywood Reporter* considered Carlton "an engaging youngster with enough acrobatic ability to make a good junior Tarzan." But the film as a whole was "one of the weakest in the series," said *Variety*.

In the fifteen months that elapsed before the release of the next Tarzan feature, several significant things occurred.

Edgar Rice Burroughs, Inc., extended Lesser's film rights to the Apeman for another twenty years. Included in the deal were eight incomplete, unpublished novels and half a dozen fragmentary plots, jotted down by ERB before his death in 1950. This extension was a direct result of another deal in which Lesser agreed to pass on ten percent of the box office earnings to ERB, Inc. Up to this point, he paid a flat annual fee of

Barker with George Macready and
Virginia Euston.

Barker with Tommy Corlton.

133

Barker with Patric Knolls.

Barker and Elmo Lincoln match ape-calls and chest-beating on the set of *Tarzan's Magic Fountain*, 1949.

134

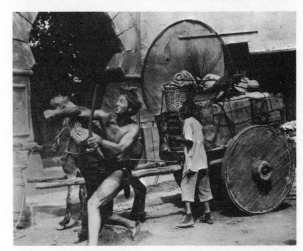

Barker with Denise Darcell in RKO's *Tarzan and the Slave Girl*, 1950.

On the set of *Tarzan's Peril.*

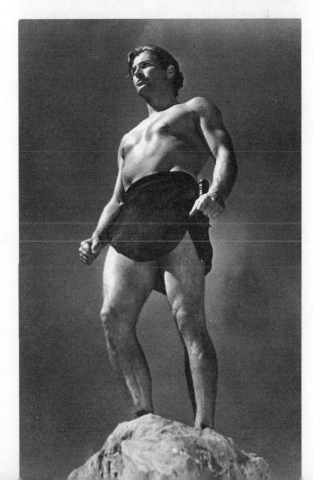

Barker with Evelyn Ankers as she had aged at the end of the filming, and Alan Napier.

Barker with Charles Drake and Albert Dekker.

$100,000 for screen rights. Under this new agreement, he would be paying about three times as much, because the average gross of his pictures was three million dollars.

At the same time, Lex Barker notified Sol Lesser that he wanted to branch out professionally. "And after expiration of my current contract with this next film," said Lex emphatically, "I'm not signing any more term contracts. If I make another Tarzan after that, it'll be strictly a one-picture deal.

"My career has reached a crisis," he continued, "It's time for a change. I'm definitely determined to get out of the jungle, although I have nothing against playing the part. Actually, I don't regret having taken the role of Tarzan, because with it I've achieved a sort of stardom which I couldn't have gained any other way."

Lex had fought for more dialogue but was frustrated, like Johnny Weissmuller had been. In an average picture, Tarzan spoke a hundred brief lines. The fact that the grosses were unusually slow on *Tarzan's Savage Fury* was attributed by Lesser to the Apeman's loquaciousness. "Tarzan had 137 lines in that one," commented the producer, "Nearly talked himself to death." To correct the error, Lesser saw to it that for the next picture, *Tarzan and the She-Devil,* Lex's lines were cut to an all-time low of eighty-three.

Barker had the ability to give a more faithful characterization to the role as ERB conceived it, but was prevented from doing so by Lesser's pedantic insistence that all his productions be imitations of Weissmuller's 1932 interpretation. What a pity that Tarzan's ten-million-dollar physique had to be burdened with a ten-cent vocabulary!

Kurt Neumann, who had served as director and associate producer on three features in the series, returned to Lesser's side to direct *Tarzan and the She-Devil.* Title of the script by Karl Kamb and Carroll Young had been *Tarzan Meets the Vampire,* but thinking it too unrealistic, Neumann had changed it, when it was the formula story he should have altered.

The she-devil of the title was the seductive Lyra (Monique Van Vooren), who, teamed with Vargo (Raymond Burr, TV's Perry Mason and Ironsides) and Fidel (Tom Conway), headed a group of ivory poachers. They kidnapped a native tribe to carry the ivory. Tarzan interfered and was

Lex Barker with Lana Turner.

captured, as was Jane, whom he believed killed. In despair, he didn't try to escape but submitted to beatings and torture until he learned that Jane was alive. Then, collecting his strength, he led his elephants in a victory stampede.

Joyce MacKenzie was Barker's Jane in *She-Devil*, his fifth in five films. Somewhat ironically, he changed mates nearly as often in real life. When he started as Tarzan in 1948, he was married to Constance Thurlow; they were divorced. In 1951 he married Arlene Dahl; they were divorced. In 1953 he married Lana Turner; they also were divorced. Alimony-ridden, he climbed off the marriage-go-round.

The reception to *Tarzan and the She-Devil* when it opened in June, 1953, was rather cool. Neal in *Variety*, explained why: "A much tamer Tarzan than heretofore cavorts in *She-Devil*, resulting in film being a tedious affair for a goodly portion of its seventy-five minutes. Only good selling points are the title and past reputation of the series. . . . Keeping the hero a tied-up captive for a long stretch just wasn't hep scripting."

*She-Devil* was Lex Barker's last Tarzan film. Lesser was not game to contract one film at a time. He had many commitments and couldn't take single-picture risks. As soon as *She-Devil* was completed, he circulated the word that he needed a new Tarzan.

Lex, typecast for adventure films, was given parts in a number of westerns. In 1956, when Kurt Neumann produced *The Deerslayer* (a version of which Jim "Tarzan" Pierce made back

Barker and Vanessa Brown.

in 1923), he remembered Lex from the Tarzan films and gave him the part.

Barker's career finally began to gain momentum. With sixteen non-Tarzan pictures behind him, he went to Europe in 1957 for a film, was a success, and stayed. Since then, Lex has made more than fifty movies all over the world: Brazil, Germany, Spain, Yugoslavia, Italy, Lebanon, and France. He has already mastered French, Spanish, Italian, and is now learning German. Although an international favorite, Lex has found his greatest success in West Germany. For the past five years, he has been the "Number One Male Star" there; his pictures, like *La Dolce Vita, Woman Times Seven,* and the *Frontiersman* series, have broken all previous box office records. In January,

1967, he was awarded Germany's Bambi Award as Best Foreign Actor of 1966.

Traveling has become a way of life for Lex, but he still hasn't grown accustomed to it. "I hate living out of a suitcase," he says, "but if you want to work in Europe, that's the way it has to be. I'm in love with Europe, so I accept the hardships."

To soften these hardships a little, Lex maintains residences in Geneva, Rome and Barcelona. His Geneva home, where he and his beautiful Spanish wife, Tita, spend most of their time, is located on the shore of Lake Geneva. His favorite pastime between films is a leisurely cruise on the lake, aboard his fifty-foot yacht "Peter Pan."

Barker struggling with Anthony Caruso while Cheetah looks on.

Barker rides the elephant.

Scott riding a wild giraffe.

Scott rides a rhinoceros.

# 14 THE JUNGLE TRAIL ENDS FOR LESSER

While in Las Vegas in 1953, two Hollywood agents, Ed and Walter Mayers, took note of a well-muscled, bronzed lifeguard named Gordon Werschkull. They brought him to the attention of Sol Lesser, who invited him to test for Tarzan.

"The six-hour screen test consisted of running, jumping, climbing trees, diving into the water, swinging on vines," Gordon later recalled, "as well as helping five girls test for the female lead." Although none of these girls came in a winner, Gordon's test was far superior to the 200 tests Sol had already conducted. The shrewd producer offered the lifeguard a seven-year contract on a modest salary (but huge compared to what he was making), with built-in fame and star-status, and a name-change to Gordon Scott.

Although his previous exposure to movie cameras was confined to having posed with Eleanor Holm, Olympic swim champ who played Jane in 1938, for a newsreel shot taken at the Sahara pool, "Gordon Scott" needed little coaxing to

accept Lesser's offer. Born August 3, 1927, in Portland, he had left Oregon University after one term in physical education to join the infantry. In short order, he earned sergeant's stripes and became a drill instructor. He specialized in close order drill, use of the rifle, bayonet and pistol, judo, and hand-to-hand combat. He later became an M.P., transporting dangerous prisoners, before his honorable discharge in 1947. Odd jobs as a fireman, cowpoke, farm machinery salesman followed before becoming a lifeguard.

The eleventh Tarzan, six-foot-three, 218-pound Gordon Scott, whose biceps measured nineteen inches, made his movie debut in *Tarzan's Hidden Jungle*, the thirtieth film in the series, and one of the weakest. The disappointing returns on *Tarzan's Savage Fury* and *Tarzan and the She-Devil* made the normally thirfty producer cut even more corners on the production budget. His penny-wise operation was most noticeable in the liberal insertion of poorly matched stock ani-

Gordon Scott was a Las Vegas lifeguard when he was chosen to be the eleventh Tarzan.

Scott on location on the Serengetti Plain in MGM's *Tarzan and the Lost Safari*, 1957.

Gordon Scott with producer Sol Lesser on the set of RKO's *Tarzan's Hidden Jungle*, 1955.

mal and jungle footage, the differences in lighting being glaringly obvious.

The story had a couple of hunters, Burger and DeGroot (Jack Elam and Charles Fredericks), trespassing in Sukulu country, where animals were held sacred. Posing as photographers, they obtained the protection of a United Nations doctor, Dr. Celliers (Peter Van Eyck), who was friendly with the Sukulu chieftain (Rex Ingram). When the hunters drove the animals across the river, where they could shoot them, the Sukulus threw the doctor and his nurse, Jill Hardy (Vera Miles) into a lion pit. Tarzan rescued them and called the animals back with his ape-call. In the stampede, the hunters were killed. And although Jane was omitted, Cheetah the chimp remained the Apeman's comedy foil.

Milton Luban, in the *Hollywood Reporter*, appraised *Hidden Jungle* as "sub-standard Tarzan filmfare. . . . The William Lively screenplay has practically no action . . . other than long walks through the jungle. Harold Schuster does as well as any director could do in staging the conversation and hiking. . . . Only noteworthy feature is the introduction of a new Tarzan, a good-looking lad with a husky physique that would make the ordinary male cut his own throat in pure frustration."

The only decent scene in the picture had Tarzan discovering Vera Miles bathing nude in the river. Actually, Vera and Gordon really discovered each other during the filming of *Hidden Jungle*, and late in 1954 they were married. It was Vera's

Scott with two pygmy women in the Ituri Forest of the Belgian Congo, during filming of *Tarzan and the Lost Safari*.

Scott and Betta St. John in the water.

Scott and Yolande Donlan on the set.

Rickie Sorenson, Eve Brent, director Bruce Humberstone, and Scott on the set of MGM's *Tarzan's Fight for Life*, 1958.

Snake-handlers rush to Scott's assistance when an 18½-foot python gets out of hand and nearly strangles the actor.

Scott with Vera Miles.

second marriage, Gordon's third. During their blissful five years together, they had one son, Mike, in 1957. But the marriage ended in divorce.

Released in February, 1955, *Tarzan's Hidden Jungle* was the last Tarzan film to be distributed by RKO-Radio Pictures, which had distributed exclusively for Sol Lesser Productions, Inc., since 1943. Early in 1956, RKO's mounting financial troubles prompted a sell-out of the company to Lucille Ball and Desi Arnaz, who converted their new holdings into Desilu Studios.

Lesser packed his belongings and approached MGM with a distribution deal. Nostalgic memories of the Weissmuller days influenced a settlement agreeable to both sides, and Sol set up camp on the Metro lot.

To celebrate what Lesser hoped would be a "new era" for the Apeman, the most ambitious plans ever were laid, with assistance from MGM. Their initial film together would be filmed on location, in full color and wide screen. Also, TV possibilities would be explored.

Lesser assembled a largely English production staff and cast at Associated British Pictures Corporated Studios in London, assigned N. Peter Rathvon, executive producer, and John Croydon, producer. Then in late 1955 he sent them off to British East Africa to shoot *Tarzan and the Lost Safari*.

The screenplay by Montgomery Pittman and Lillie Hayward made sense and had a minimum of the jungle humor that overtakes most writers when confronted with a chimp in the cast. The story: When an airplane crashed in the jungle,

144

Scott with Vera Miles, Peter Van Eyck, and Rex Ingram.

Tarzan rescued the five passengers (Yolande Donlan, Betta St. John, Wilfrid Hyde White, Peter Arne and George Confouris) and agreed to lead them to the coast. They were joined by a treacherous white hunter, Tusker Hawkins (Robert Beatty), who tried to sell the group to the Oparian chieftain (Orlando Martins) for ivory. The party was captured by the Oparians and nearly sacrificed to the Lion God, but Tarzan saved them.

Location shooting in Technicolor was done near Murchison Falls in Uganda, in the Kilimanjaro Mountains on the border of Kenya and Tanganyika, and in the Belgian Congo. Fourteen different African tribes added atmosphere, as did wild animals in their native environment. This was the first time that action scenes were filmed in Africa. When *Tarzan's Peril* was on location, the footage acquired was mostly background, with practically nothing acted out by the stars.

Scott with Peter Arne, Wilfred Hyde-White, Yoland Donland, George Coulouris, and Betta St. John.

Tarzan gets a stranglehold on an Oparian.

Scott, a rugged outdoorsman, felt at ease in Africa and was intrigued by the wild animals and the different tribes. After two days of work with the Masai tribe in Tanganyika, a Masai warrior nicknamed Scott Mtu Ule Na Panda Miti Mineju, that is, the Warrior Who Climbs Tall Trees. The muscular Scott then earned the respect of several tribes by outhurling a giant Wakomba in a spear-throwing match. And on a bet, to the astonishment of the natives, he demonstrated his cowboying experience by catching and riding a wild giraffe for five minutes.

His only misfortune came with a lion that had been raised by a woman in Tanganyika. It weighed about 500 pounds and had a big black mane. For more than a month he worked with the animal and became good pals—he thought. "Then one day when, as I reached to pet the beast, his mistress called him," Scott recollected, "and seeing my hand outstretched, apparently thought I meant to keep him from answering the call. He sprang at me and tore my leg open and I had to have thirty-two stitches taken. This only goes to show that wild animals are never really tame."

As in *Tarzan's Hidden Jungle*, Jane was absent from the picture. And even with two gorgeous gals on the safari, Tarzan had no romantic involvement. The fast and realistic direction of Bruce Humberstone emphasized action and suspense rather than romance.

Metro's release of *Tarzan and the Lost Safari* on March 25, 1957, marked their first Apeman film distribution in fifteen years. Being one of the series' best since Metro's last Tarzan in 1942, *Lost Safari* merited handling by the studio that gave first life to the Apeman in talkies.

"*Tarzan and the Lost Safari* is probably going to be seen only by fans of the series," surmised the *Hollywood Reporter* film critic, James Powers, "and in a way this is too bad. Because it is a good picture." "Technical credits generally are above average," affirmed Whit. in *Variety*.

During the months that *Lost Safari* was on location in Africa, Sol Lesser formed a Tarzan TV company with telefilm producer Jack Denove, to do a series for NBC. No sooner had the announcement of the pending series been made than a suit was filed against Lesser. Walter White, of Commodore Productions, who had produced the then current Tarzan radio show and handled world distribution of it, claimed that he had the TV rights to Tarzan by an agreement with ERB, Inc., dated December 20, 1950. Apparently, White's exclusive world distribution rights to the radio show granted him first refusal rights to any TV series because of the growing television threat to radio. NBC, not wanting to get caught in the middle, reneged on all commitments with Lesser, promising to re-open negotiations after the mess was cleared up.

In spite of Lesser's claim that he had cleared

Scott issues the ape-call.

the TV rights, running full-page ads in the trade papers reproducing a letter from ERB, Inc., White sued. Always trying to stay ahead of the game, Lesser agreed to settle out of court. He offered first refusal rights to White, his acceptance of which would have called for his financing production, an expense which would have been prohibitive for his meager company. White refused and protested, threatening another suit. But Lesser stood his ground, insisting that he had met the conditions of the contract, and suggested a possible cash settlement.

Following litigations which held up TV plans until 1958, Lesser finally paid White off. For a family television series, Lesser agreed with director Bruce Humberstone and producer Jack Denove that Jane and Boy must be resurrected. Eve Brent, a girl from Fort Worth, Texas, was handed Jane's leather tunic. Critic Jack Moffit found her "so softly pink and golden-haired that she seemed to have swung into the jungle straight from the chorus line in Las Vegas."

With Boy, they ran into the same problem that Lesser encountered when he gave Lex Barker a young counterpart, Joey, in *Tarzan's Savage Fury*. Tarzan's new son was called Tartu, which seems to be an elision of "Tarzan-two." His origin was not explained; was merely introduced in publicity releases as "the couple's ten-year-old adopted son, played by Rickie Sorenson."

Conferences with writer Thomas Hal Phillips produced an inherently slow screenplay called *Tarzan's Fight for Life*, which was to introduce the new Tarzan family and celebrate the fortieth anniversary of the Apeman in films. Also resulting were three or four TV pilot scripts.

Contrary to advertisements of *Tarzan's Fight*

*for Life* that read "Filmed Where it Happens," the Metrocolor picture was shot at the MGM Culver City studios. Much footage, however, from the previous journey to Africa was interlaced throughout. The hack plot concerned Tarzan's efforts to aid Dr. Sturdy (Carl Benton Reid) to operate a modern hospital in the jungle, which was strenuously opposed by a witch doctor, Futa (James Edwards), and a native warrior, Ramo (ex-football-star Woody Strode). The usual cliché kidnappings, race against time for serum, capture and escape of Tarzan, and triumph of modern medicine over black magic, all take place before picture's end.

One better-than-average sequence showed Scott wrestling with a live, eighteen-and-a-half foot python, which required six men to unravel it from Tarzan's body at the conclusion of the scene. It nearly strangled Scott.

Completion of *Fight for Life* was immediately followed by the filming of three TV pilots. Optimistically, Lesser solicited for a sponsor through NBC. Collectively, he, NBC, and Denove were unsuccessful in selling the series. These pilot films were eventually edited together into a feature called *Tarzan and the Trappers* which had its world premiere on television on May 5, 1966. Telecast in black and white, Tarzan encountered an irresponsible animal trapper (Lesley Bradley) and an unscrupulous game warden in the first part; then went in search of a lost city.

Frustrated and disappointed that his most ambitious effort didn't meet expectations, Lesser entertained an offer from two new young producers named Sy Weintraub and Harvey Hayutin to buy Sol Lesser Productions and the Tarzan rights that went with it. The poor reviews and meagre grosses of *Tarzan's Fight for Life* after its release in July, 1958, convinced Lesser that maybe he should sell. It was a difficult decision to make; after all, he had been involved with Tarzan since 1931 and had produced fifteen features, one serial and some TV pilots. But the series was at its lowest ebb. Perhaps the property was exhausted. Furthermore, Lesser's having suffered a heart attack was a strongly persuasive factor in favor of selling.

Acting quickly, before nostalgia could overpower him, he called Weintraub and Hayutin to make a deal. For his production company's phy-

sical assets, all Tarzan properties including past films, and the TV and motion picture rights to the character, Lesser was paid something over two million dollars. Scott's contract and loincloth were also part of the bargain.

Sy Weintraub, an ex-TV producer and originator of the concept of the Late Show, had been, among other things, vice-president of Motion Pictures for Television, Inc., the largest supplier of films for TV. Impulsively selling his TV interests, he moved from New York to Hollywood and formed a partnership with Harvey Hayutin to buy

Scott and Eve Brent.

the rights to Tarzan. The series he felt was dying; Tarzan's image had disintegrated. He meant to modernize Tarzan, adding a little of his rightful dignity, long lost in the transition from book to film. Weintraub was certain that Tarzan could make a lot of money with the proper managing.

After his divorce from the Tarzan films, Sol Lesser became deeply involved in the unfortunate Hollywood Museum, which died for lack of administrative leadership and civic support. In September, 1967, the seventy-nine-year-old pioneer producer joined the University of Southern California's Department of Cinema as an adjunct professor. He is teaching a course on "The Motion Picture Producer, his Organization and Responsibilities." Well qualified to teach such a course, Lesser as an independent producer turned out several hundred films in his career, which began in 1906 as an ice-cream vendor in his father's San Francisco nickelodeon. His USC course is limited to twelve graduate students and meets twice weekly.

Reminiscing often about the Tarzan films, he feels that his contribution has been major to keeping the character alive in pictures. He takes note of the current Tarzans and says, "Maybe I shouldn't have sold him. I wish I still had Tarzan to keep me active."

But then, Sol Lesser, ideally suited for the job once, is as much a part of a bygone era as he considered Big Jim Pierce to be back in 1933.

Miller with Joanna Barnes.

# 15 TARZAN THE WORST

At about the same time as Weintraub and Hayutin were working out arrangements for their first Tarzan film, MGM producer Al Zimbalist announced that they were going to remake their 1932 classic, *Tarzan the Apeman*. Zimbalist's father was Sam Zimbalist, a successful producer who had started his career in 1939 with *Tarzan Finds a Son*. Studio interest in the Apeman, which had died in 1942, had been rekindled with Lesser's two productions for them.

A strong objection came from Weintraub, insisting that he was the only one who had authority to produce a new Tarzan epic. Metro paid no heed to his lawsuit threats and informed him that they were infringing on no one's territory. As on all their early productions, MGM retained remake rights to their initial Tarzan feature. Unable to stop them, Weintraub returned to his own plans for the Apeman, resolved that MGM would nowhere figure in them in the future. MGM director Joseph Newman's choice for Tarzan in their re-make was Denny Miller, former UCLA basketball sensation, who turned down pro

offers to be an actor, Miller, twenty-four, was a six-foot-four, 212-pound studio contractee who had been Metro property since his senior year at UCLA, where his father was a physical education instructor. Miller's break was the typical Hollywood fairy tale that just doesn't happen. He had been discovered on Sunset Boulevard by agent Bob Raison while working as a furniture mover to put himself through school. "Very impressive physically," Raison remembers. "So I took him around to the studios; Metro signed him."

Playing Jane to Miller's debut role as the first blond Tarzan was lovely Joanna Barnes, a Phi Beta Kappa graduate of Smith College, who, even more than Brenda Joyce, reminded fans of Maureen O'Sullivan's tender quality. The parts originally played by Neil Hamilton and C. Aubrey Smith were given to Cesare Danova and Robert Douglas.

The 1932 screenplay was recognizable only in general action in the adaptation by Robert F. Hill, whose first contact with the Tarzan series dated to 1921.

151

MGM's *Tarzan the Ape Man*, 1959. Joanna Barnes, a new Jane, and Dennis Miller, a new Tarzan.

Dennis Miller with Joanna Barnes in MGM's *Tarzan the Ape Man*.

Miller and Cheetah.

Dennis Miller, the twelfth Tarzan, issues the ape-call.

153

Dennis Miller as a U.C.L.A. basketball star in 1957.

Usually, re-makes are inferior to the original work. *Tarzan the Apeman,* released in October, 1959, was no exception. In spite of MGM's publicity about it being a big-budget picture, it was a cheapie.

Mostly, the action from the 1932 version repeated itself; to the extent that large chunks of the original footage were interpolated into the new film and tinted to match the color. And as incredible as it seems, nearly all vine-swinging scenes, with Johnny Weissmuller easily identified, were lifted from the original *Apeman.* So were the scenes of elephants wrecking the pygmy village. All of the pygmies were carefully edited out of this borrowed film because, in sparing costs, the pygmies in the 1959 version were Negro kids from Fairfax High School in Los Angeles. The driving energy and integrity of Irving Thalberg that had in 1932 insured authenticity by locating and using real pygmies and dwarfs was gone.

In fact, the principals in this new film were dressed in wardrobe left over from *King Solomon's Mines* and given a Watusi companion so that stock shots from that notable film could be used. And, lo and behold, the famous crocodile fight from *Tarzan and his Mate* showed up in a new tinted glory.

154

The crowning blow was that Miller was not even once called Tarzan, or referred to as Tarzan, in the film—a gross oversight.

This patched-together, crazy-quilt quickie was a film editor's nightmare, beneficial only to Miller as his screen bow. And Miller, jittery about watching himself on the screen, never saw *Apeman.* But Vern Coriell, critic and fan alike, wrote in the *Burroughs Bulletin:* "The less said about this film the better. I've not talked with one Burroughs enthusiast who had anything good to say about it. MGM enjoyed the reputation of making the best of the Tarzan series . . . until now."

In the twenty months that Denny Miller was under contract to Metro, his only work was eight weeks on *Apeman.* "I felt a little embarrassed at drawing a $175 weekly." said Denny.

Once free from MGM, Denny started doing guest shots in TV shows like *Riverboat, G. E. Theater, Laramie,* and others. On a visit to Revue Studios, with Bob Raison, the big, amiable, eager-to-learn young actor caught the attention of producer Howard Christie, who made him a regular on his *Wagon Train* TV series. Christie changed Denny's name to Scott Miller and gave him the role of Duke Shannon, a young frontiersman. The intent was to build Miller to step into Robert Horton's co-starring spot in case the termperamental actor left the show. After a lengthy personality clash between Horton and the network, Horton departed for "more rewarding roles" and Miller became the co-star with John McIntire, who had stepped in for Ward Bond after his death. They continued on the show for nearly four years.

In the 1965-66 TV season, Miller was in a new series, *Mona McKluskey*, as the husband of Juliet Prowse; and his name was back to Denny Miller. More recently, he has been doing guest parts on TV series like *I Spy, Run for your Life*, and *Gilligan's Island*, among others. He has also completed featured roles in *The Party*, with Peter Sellers and Claudine Longet, and *Armageddon*, with Mala Powers and Henry Wilcoxen. *Armageddon* probably won't be ready for release until early 1969.

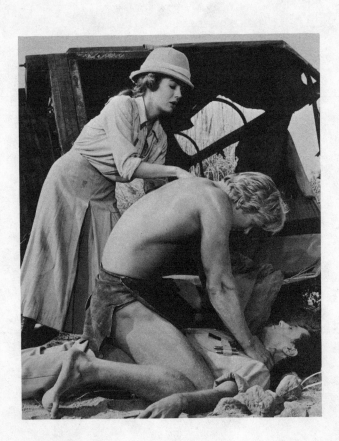

Scott and Cheetah.

# 16 TARZAN THE BEST

The October, 1959, release of *Tarzan the Ape-man* had been preceded by the July opening of *Tarzan's Greatest Adventure*, Weintraub's first entry into the series. Following his momentary pre-production clash with MGM, Weintraub had proceeded with Hayutin to produce a new kind of Tarzan film.

Poring over the past pictures, Weintraub had noticed that the most successful recent film, *Tarzan and the Lost Safari*, had been filmed entirely on location, and with British technicians. That seemed to be the ticket. Entering into a "cooperation" with East African Film Services, they set off on a filming safari to the Kikuyu country in Kenya.

When they arrived in Nairobi and star Gordon Scott stepped off the plane, a myriad of youngsters surrounded him, clamoring to carry his luggage. Scott picked one small fellow who, in awe, declared, "You big. Built like tree." Amused, Scott smiled. "You strong like lion," continued the boy, walking away, "You carry own luggage." And Scott did.

Interjecting new ideas and new blood on the production side, Weintraub made *Greatest Adventure* the initial departure from the established series format. Sy decided he had to get adults, particularly women, interested in Tarzan. Out went Jane. With her went the safaris and the cornshuck scripts that were not written so much as grunted.

British director John Guillerman, who concocted the screenplay with Berne Giler, based on an original story by Les Crutchfield, was not entirely certain of how to make the character of Tarzan contemporary within the trend towards realism. Prodded by Weintraub's vision, they took the Apeman from the grunt and groan stage and made him literate, but still prone to chest-beating and ape-calls. Their screen treatment, aided by the expert editing of Bert Rule, provided a ninety-minute straight-line film narrative that moved. It was tightly knit, without a single foot of wasted film.

*Greatest Adventure*'s quick-paced action was supplemented with violence and, in the absence

157

Gordon Scott and Jock Mahoney in Paramount's *Tarzan the Magnificent*, 1960.

Scott arriving at the Nairobi airport.

Anthony Quayle, Sean Connery (long before James Bond appeared), and Scilla Gabel in *Tarzan's Greatest Adventure*, 1959.

158

of the wholesome Jane, a pair of sexpots; a sultry Italian (Scilla Gabel) for the villains and a saucy blonde aviatrix, Angie (Sara Shane), as the romantic interest for Scott. The "coming attractions" for the picture boasted a torchy kissing scene between Tarzan and his leading lady, which was deleted from the final print.

The villains were four diverse British types: Slade (Anthony Quayle), Kruger (Niall McGinnis), O'Bannion (Sean Connery), and Dino (Al Mulock). In raiding a settlement for explosives to use in a diamond mine, they practically wiped it out. And Tarzan, discovering the atrocity, pursued them upriver to their mine.

Sixty percent of *Greatest Adventure* was filmed in Africa, the interiors in a London studio. Although Jane was out, Sy had hoped to keep Cheetah in. He carted two chimpanzees from England to Kenya, where the terrified chimps froze up, in spite of the special cage that was built to shut out scary jungle night noises. (Sol Lesser could have told him that.) So he used one of them exactly long enough for Tarzan to say, "So long, Cheetah."

Another problem Weintraub encountered in Kenya was a strike by the 300 Kikuyu tribesmen being employed as extras. They made four demands: shorter hours, free posho (a porridge), higher wages, and freedom from England. He conceded the first three.

Philip K. Scheuer, reviewing for the *Los Angeles Times,* hailed *Tarzan's Greatest Adventure* as a "unique adult tale in Cinemascope . . . I would single it out for its impact, even brilliance, as cinema-making. . . . The influence may well be that of these British technicians (who) obviously have not lost the traditional Maugham-like knack for storytelling."

Hoping to minimize the setback that the new Tarzan suffered from the four-month-later showings of MGM's *Apeman* re-hash, Weintraub began production without delay on his second image-reshaping film, *Tarzan the Magnificent.* It, like his first, was shot in Eastman color in Kenya and London as a Weintraub-Hayutin Production.

The shooting script was developed by Berne Giler again, in collaboration with Robert Day, who also directed and assisted Sy with the casting. Scott continued as Tarzan; Betta St. John, who had been a member of Lesser's *Lost Safari* cast, made a return appearance to the series.

Since there were four heavies in the story, Weintraub contacted the actors who had done such a splendid job in *Greatest Adventure.* Of-

fered another part, Sean Connery was apologetic: "Two fellows took an option on me for some spy picture, and are exercising it. But I'll be in your next," he promised, having no idea what would happen with James Bond. For his part in *Greatest Adventure,* he earned $5,600; his last Bond film, *You Only Live Twice* (1967), brought him $350,000.

Weintraub also lost Anthony Quayle. Director David Lean saw Quayle's performance in *Greatest Adventure* and assigned him a role in *Lawrence of Arabia.* The only returning heavy was Al Mulock.

*Tarzan the Magnificent* chronicled Tarzan's treacherous journey through the jungle to the authorities with his prisoner, Coy Banton (Jock Mahoney). They took off on foot when the river boat they were going to take was blown up by Banton's father, Abel (John Carradine) and brothers, Martin (Mulock), Johnny (Gary Cockrell), and Ethan (Ron MacDonnell). Five of the boat's passengers—Tate, a Negro engineer (Earl Cameron), Ames (Lionel Jeffries), his wife Fay (Miss St. John), Conway (Charles Tingwell), and Laurie (Alexandra Stewart)—all had such good reasons to go with Tarzan that he couldn't refuse. Thus encumbered, Tarzan set off, the Bantons at his heels.

As in *Greatest Adventure,* Jane was omitted and sex given freer reign; but Tarzan himself had no romantic involvement. And, happily, Cheetah's role was all but eliminated again. The most unusual thing about *Tarzan the Magnificent* was the absence of the Tarzan yell for the first time since sound motion pictures. Some fans disliked the omission, but considering the widespread use of the ape-call for laughs in variety shows, the producer acted wisely.

Released in July, 1960, *Tarzan the Magnificent* was distributed by Paramount, as *Greatest Adventure* had been. Late critic Maurice B. Gardner rated it "one of the best Tarzan films to date. Reviewers hailed *Tarzan's Greatest Adventure* as the greatest; but *Magnificent* is just a little better —so the producers have scored again. . . . Let's hope still more films of this exceptional high calibre will be forthcoming. I am positive were

Sean Connery and Anthony Quayle in *Tarzan's Greatest Adventure.*

Scott and Sara Shane.

Scott with Alexandra Stewart, Charles Tingwell, Betta St. John, and Lionel Jeffries.

Burroughs alive today, he would fully agree that the Tarzan films are getting better and that Gordon Scott makes a truly magnificent Apeman." Saul Ostrov called it "outstanding!" And the trade papers appraised the film as "impressive!"

*Tarzan's Greatest Adventure* and *Tarzan the Magnificent* were both fast-moving, action films, probably the two best Tarzans ever made. Outside of the high technical quality, their success is due greatly to Weintraub's vision, but in no lesser way to Scott's excellent characterization. Although generally civilized through the second film, Scott reverted realistically and believably to the primitive when the situation demanded it.

Following *Magnificent*, Scott checked in his loincloth and hunting knife at Weintraub's request. There were two years left on Scott's contract, but Weintraub's streamlining of the Tarzan image had just begun. He wanted to make the Apeman leaner and to get away from the muscle-bound weight-lifter concept. Scott, always easygoing, cooperated.

The best screen Tarzan disappeared from the Hollywood scene. A year or so later, he reappeared in Rome in a couple of Italian spectaculars, *Duel of the Titans* (1963) with Steve Reeves, and *Samson and the Seven Miracles of the World* (1963). Many others, like *Goliath* and *The Vampires* (1964), followed. Becoming quite a sensation in Europe he embarked on a second acting career there and was last seen in an Italian western, *The Tramplers* (1968).

Big fight between Scott and Jock Mahoney.

163

Jock Mahoney and Woody Strode in MGM's *Tarzan's Three Challenges,* 1963.

# 17 THE NEW IMAGE

An even dozen Tarzans had come and gone. And Sy Weintraub was in no hurry to cast number thirteen. With no immediate commitments, the ambitious, youngish man of thirty-eight took time to reorganize his business.

As a beginning, he bought out his partner, Harvey Hayutin, and renamed his company Banner Productions. In the two years since he had become Tarzan's mentor, he had come a long way. As head of his own company, he was going to be completely independent. He said then: "What I'm trying to set up is an independent operation with maneuverability, a totally self-contained umbrella, with our own financing and production. And later, with television, our own distributing."

His first two Tarzan films taught him a great deal about the advantages of overseas production. "When we go into a foreign country, it is like a guerrilla operation; our tools are the people of that land. We manage with one-third the size of a domestic crew by using local labor. Thus, we are able to shoot a Tarzan picture for one million plus.

"Then there's the added incentive of using a different, exciting locale each time. I'd like to do something in Peru, or India, perhaps. What makes Tarzan such a great property is that he's international; every country thinks he belongs to them. Actually, he's English, the son of a lord, but that's forgotten now.

"What shouldn't be forgotten is that fifty percent of our profits are made abroad. And in the making of any future Tarzans, I want to stress the international aspect, make Tarzan somewhat of a world traveler. His films should be geared to the universal market and not so much for American consumption."

Intent on proving his theories, Sy Weintraub set his sights on India as the location for the next Tarzan film. His director was John Guillermin, who had proven his ability on *Greatest Adventure* and on several MGM comedies and adventure films. Guillermin worked with Robert

Jock Mahoney, the thirteenth Tarzan, feeds a baby elephant on location in India in MGM's *Tarzan Goes To India,* 1962.

Tarzan shows fantastic strength in holding off two oxen and trying to pull them apart.

Hardy Andrews on the screenplay, descriptively called *Tarzan Goes to India*.

But who for the lead? Weintraub had the answer. He saw Tarzan as leaner, taller, and more agile than Gordon Scott had been. In his mind, he had chosen Scott's successor upon seeing the first rushes from *Tarzan the Magnificent*. The arch-heavy in that picture was six-foot-four, 220-pound Jock Mahoney, an athletic former stunt man. Mahoney got the nod to become the thirteenth actor to don the loincloth.

Mahoney's acquaintance with Tarzan went back to the time Johnny Weissmuller bowed out from the part. He was tested for Weissmuller's replacement, as were others, like Willard Parker.

"I lost out to Lex Barker," Jock mused then, "but, like Bruce Bennett, I got the part after all. I'm luckier, though, than Barker was. He had to work with a chimp. There's not going to be a Jane or Cheetah in this one. I'm glad the chimp's gone. They're the dirtiest, meanest animals to work with."

Born in Chicago on February 7, 1919, Mahoney, who was christened Jacques O'Mahoney, is French and Irish, with a strain of Cherokee Indian. While attending the University of Iowa, he excelled in swimming, basketball, and football. In 1941, with two years of college behind him, he quit to join the war effort. He served as a Marine fighter pilot and instructor.

Following the war, he went to Hollywood and, after a brief stint as a horsebreeder, became an ace stuntman doubling for stars like Gregory Peck, Errol Flynn, John Wayne, and others. Realizing that the stuntman doesn't walk off into the sunset with the heroine, he tried acting. Earning a reputation in westerns, he was signed by Gene Autry for the lead in the popular *Range Rider* TV series; his seventy-eight half-hour episodes have been since syndicated all over the world. More recently, he starred in a number of adventure films for Universal-International. And for a couple of seasons he played Yancy Derringer on CBS-TV before going to work for Weintraub.

For *Tarzan Goes to India*, Jock insisted on doing all of his own stunts, such as riding elephants, getting jerked into the air upside down in an animal snare, and wrestling a live leopard. "I couldn't ask a stuntman to do something," says Jock, "that I wouldn't do myself."

In color and Cinemascope, *Tarzan Goes to India* was filmed in the legendary jungles of Mysore Province, in Bangalore, Bombay, and Madras.

To find an Indian girl for the female lead, Weintraub advertised in a Bombay daily paper and was swamped with 800 applicants. A dark-eyed gal named Simi, daughter of a Brigadier General in the Indian Army, was selected to make her film debut.

Simi, as Princess Kamara, initiated the film's action by sending for Tarzan to help save 300 elephants that would be drowned when a great dam was opened, forming a man-made lake and powering an electric plant. The head engineer, Bryce (Leo Gordon), and O'Hara (Mark Dana) were the nasties, ignoring the problem and obstructing the Apeman, who, in triumph, failed again to voice the cry of the bull-ape.

With the basic plot established, Weintraub felt that, since both Jane and Cheetah were gone, perhaps a little boy should be added for family appeal. Searching the streets of Bombay, they found an Indian lad named Jai. He became Jai the elephant boy for the picture, in which he befriended Tarzan and helped round up the elephants for a stampede out of the valley before it was flooded.

The rhythmic and exotic musical score for *Tarzan Goes to India* was composed and arranged by international favorite Ravi Shankar and Jaipishhan. They are India's top composing team, with more than 120 pictures to their credit.

During the two months on location, there was one minor incident. One weekend, the Indians

Mahoney faces a killer cobra during the filming of *Tarzan Goes to India*.

Mahoney with Feroz Kahn, Mark Dana, and Simi, a well-known Indian actress.

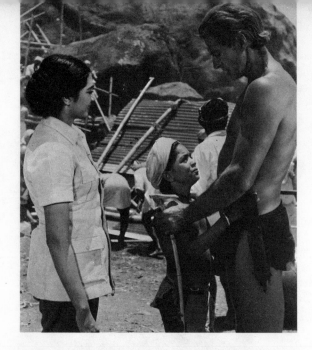

informed Guillermin that they would not be working on the following Monday because the stars showed that the world was coming to an end. The following Tuesday, they were back at work as usual. When asked why the world hadn't ended on Monday, they replied that the calamity had been warded off with prayers and *sagnas*. That was why they needed the time off.

When *Tarzan Goes to India* went into release in July, 1962, Metro-Goldwyn-Mayer did the distributing. Disregarding their differences in 1959, Weintraub had made a deal with them because of their extensive distribution system and familiarity with the product.

Despite the fact that *Tarzan Goes to India* was a weaker film than either of Weintraub's first two, and that Mahoney, although athletically fit, came across too lean for the Apeman, it was the biggest commercial success in Tarzan history. Metro alone netted a million dollars plus for their minimum troubles. A *Los Angeles Herald-Examiner* review read: "Juvenile action fans are in for a treat as they watch tree-swinging Jock Mahoney go to work."

Francis Wyndham, writing for the *London Sunday Times*, was among the first to notice that "Sy Weintraub's tactics have brought about a Tarzan revival."

His theories strengthened, Sy Weintraub's formula began to fall into place. For Tarzan's next adventure, he decided on the exotic jungles of Thailand.

The seeming success of the little boy in *Tarzan Goes to India* inspired Berne Giler and director

Robert Day, both of whom were veterans of at least one previous Tarzan picture, to write a screenplay in which the action revolved around a small boy. Titled *Tarzan's Three Challenges,* the plot involved the summoning of the Apeman to an oriental country to protect the young spiritual heir, Kashi (Ricky Der), whose throne was in danger of being ursurped by the former spiritual leader's evil brother, Khan (Woody Strode).

Strode played a dual role as both the dying spiritual leader and his brother, who, in the course of the action, had to face Tarzan in three tests of strength. In the third, a sabre-swinging duel while balancing on a net stretched above vats of boiling oil, he loses his life. The young Prince's nursemaid, Cho San, was portrayed by an oriental actress, Tsuruko Kobayashi.

The chimp was still absent, and in a probable effort to supply some of the comic relief for which he had been responsible, a baby elephant named Hungry was added to the cast. According to publicity releases: "The endearing baby elephant becomes a devoted and, on occasion, strategically helpful ally of Tarzan and Kashi." Actually, the little pachyderm ate up a lot of good footage that would have been more worthwhile had it been devoted to scenery. "Cute" animal antics had been overdone with the chimp; the elephant was a poor substitute.

Most of the location shooting took place near Bangkok and in the jungle area of Chieng-Mai, eleven miles south of the Chinese border. A sacred Thailand shrine, the Temple of Buddha's Footprint, was photographed for the first time in a movie. Crew members removed their shoes before entering and worked in almost complete silence.

Tarzan as cameraman on location in Thailand.

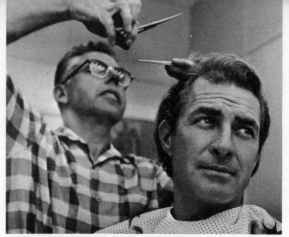

Jock Mahoney gets a haircut.

Inside another temple, that of Watsaunddock, a sequence was filmed against a 500-year-old, forty-foot high gold Buddha, which was surrounded by a dozen smaller hand-carved Buddhas.

It is likely that *Three Challenges* was the most visually arresting of the entire series. There were great processions led by jeweled elephants; panoramic views of the Thailand's ancient and mysterious cities and jungles; a thousand native girls performing the "dance of the candles"; all photographed in Metrocolor and expansive Dyalscope.

Halfway through production, Mahoney contracted amoebic dysentery and dengue fever, which led to pneumonia. He dropped from 220 pounds to 175 during his illness. Manfully finishing his role, he looked emaciated and terribly

Jock Mahoney rides the elephant.

worn at the end. In fact, the film strained credibility when the weakened Mahoney bested the powerfully built Strode.

"Although he {Mahoney} seems to lack something of the weight and heft of the earlier Tarzans," reported the *Motion Picture Herald* when *Tarzan's Three Challenges* opened in June, 1963, "he is certainly sufficiently active, strong and ruggedly handsome to satisfy. . . . Director Robert Day succeeded admirably in creating an exciting, imaginative tale, especially suited for the youngsters." Critic Maurice B. Gardner was less reserved in his praise, writing, "This is one of the most strikingly beautiful films in the forty-five-year history of Tarzan movies. . . . If you've been passing them up, this time don't."

In the conferences that ensued after returning to the States, Jock Mahoney retired from the jungle scene. He needed time to recuperate; it took him a year and a half to regain the weight he lost.

Besides, Weintraub felt that Jock was a little too old to fit in with his plans. Looking forward to a television series, Sy wanted a young man who could grow with the show. Jock, at forty-four, had already reached his peak. He wasn't a good prospect for TV. By mutual agreement, the remainder of Jock's contract was dissolved. At the same time, Weintraub entered in a new agreement with Edgar Rice Burroughs, Inc., giving him rights to the Tarzan character until 1972.

For the next few months, Mahoney took it easy. Becoming active again, he went back to making adventure films, like *California* (1963) *The Walls of Hell* (1964), *Moro Witch Doctor* (1965), and others. He has also worked on several *Tarzan* TV episodes for Weintraub.

His step-daughter Sally Field, by his marriage to actress Margaret Field, is "The Flying Nun" on the ABC-TV network.

# 18 BODY BY MICHAELANGELO

While completing his first four pictures, a formula evolved out of Weintraub's concept of a successful Tarzan. "Unlike other formulas," he said, "it is adequately variable, and unrestrive enough to avoid becoming stale: (1) a reasonably believable situation; (2) a young Burt Lancaster cast as Tarzan; (3) with the action someplace in the world where Tarzan hasn't been shot before."

Weintraub had already carted camera and crew to many locales around the world—East Africa, Kenya, India, and Thailand. Consistently, from location, the cast and production team adjourned to London studios for indoor scenes and "post-dubbing." That is, all sound is added after the picture's completion. Producer Weintraub is proud of his method: "We've given a new technique to the industry. We shoot nearly everything on location. And silent. In working with animals, trainers yell commands. And birds, overhead planes, and local inhabitants are all troublesome to the sound man. We eliminate all such interference by post-dubbing. Plus, we avoid high maintenance costs

of a domestic studio by location shooting. It is a difficult but rewarding process."

For his next, Weintraub looked southward to Acapulco, where *Tarzan and the Mermaids* had been shot some fifteen years earlier.

The search for a "young Burt Lancaster" who would be compatible with both TV and motion picture arrangements continued for eighteen months. After discounting over 300 applicants, among whom were Olympic pole-vaulter Don Bragg and New York Giants halfback Frank Gifford, Weintraub decided on Mike Henry, the superbly muscled, Los Angeles Rams star linebacker. Henry's 228-pounds were distributed over his six-foot-three steam-roller frame as though by the hands of Michaelangelo. And his rugged, attractive features surprisingly resembled cartoon artist Hal Foster's comic strip version of the Apeman.

An avid Rams fan, Weintraub had watched Mike play many times. Quite by chance, Sy saw a TV documentary about the Rams called *Men*

Mike Henry, the fourteenth Tarzan, in AIP's *Valley of Gold*, 1966.

Mike Henry slides down in Paramount's *Tarzan and the Jungle Boy*, 1968.

*From the Boys*, which had been produced by Mike and featured him.

"The next thing you know," Mike said, "we're in his office talking deals. We did a screen test. It turned out real good and we drew up the papers." Accepting Weintraub's lucrative offer to make him "wealthier than a whole backfield," Henry withdrew from the violent world of football that he had known for seven years, three with the Pittsburgh Steelers and four with the Rams. His temporary retirement from the sports scene became permanent on July 24, 1965, when Weintraub decided that football was going to interfere with his plans.

Mike, Los Ángeles-born in 1937, had already had some acting experience. Under contract to Warner Brothers Studios from 1961 to 1964, he had parts on TV shows like *Surfside Six*, *Hawai-*

174

Mike Henry with Steve Bond, the most recent Boy.

Henry with Ron Gams, and Alicia Gure.

*ian Eye,* and *Cheyenne,* and a film, *Spencer's Mountain* (1963).

Before Sy would let Mike debut as the Jungle Lord, he had to shed twenty pounds from his legs and waist. A slimmer Henry made preparations with Weintraub and company to sail to Acapulco to begin filming January 25, 1965, on *Tarzan '65.* Retitled *Tarzan '66,* the picture was finally released in June, 1966, as *Tarzan and the Valley of Gold.* The original titles stemmed from Weintraub's desire to alert the movie-going public to the fact that the Apeman had been updated. Character refinements that had begun with Gordon Scott in 1959 and were carried through Mahoney's films were coming to a head.

In Mexico, Tarzan Henry donned a lightweight summer suit and became the James Bond of the jungle. After arriving in a helicopter, he gunned it out with the no-goodniks in O.K. Corral fashion in Mexico City's Plaza de Toros.

To give Tarzan new sex appeal, his loincloth shrunk to a mini-cloth; and Jane remained on the cutting room floor, gathering dust. Producer Weintraub had cut the Apeman's character to the bone and redressed it, largely according to Burroughs' recipe. Tarzan became a well-mannered, soft-spoken gentleman ape who was at home in a Parisian nightclub as in the treetops. He was hip to the modern world, could do the Watusi at the better discotheques, and got the girl at the end, because he was, in summary, a "new embodiment of culture."

But something was missing. There was nothing savage about him anymore; even in the jungle he was a gentleman. No longer was he *Tarzan the Terrible* who, pleased with the scent of death, placed his foot on his kill in a head-tossing, chest-pounding frenzy, culminating in the ape-call of triumph.

Weintraub contended that below the surface, his Apeman "is still primitive. When Tarzan kills, he is a worse killer than his enemy. And like Rousseau's natural man, he stays in the jungle because he wants to. Not because he has to."

To insure that Tarzan be presented properly, well-known adventure writer Clair Huffaker was signed to write the script. The plot, as in Mahoney's films, was built around a small boy, ten-year-old Ramel (Manuel Padilla, Jr.), who was kidnapped because he was believed to be the sole link to a lost city of gold. The kidnapper was international criminal Vinaro (David Opatashu), whose hobby was sending explosive watches to his enemies. His bodyguard was the mountainous Mr. Train (six-foot-six Don Megowan, a´ la Yul Brynner), who proved no match for Tarzan in a death struggle. Accompanying them, by force, was voluptuous Sophia Renault (Nancy Kovack, who replaced the equally voluptuous Sharon Tate in the role). Sophia was later left to die with an explosive around her neck, but was rescued by the Apeman.

*Valley of Gold* marked the return of the chimpanzee. The chimp, called Dinky, a cantankerous veteran performer, joined a lion and jaguar in helping Tarzan track Vinaro's army of tanks and helicopters that made their way to the lost city.

Director Robert Day, now a member of the Banner production staff, heroically supervised the ten weeks of shooting in the jungles surrounding Acapulco, in the Chapultepec Castle, the Aztec ruins at Teotihuacan and the giant caves of Guerro; and the interiors and dubbing at studios in Churubusco.

While shooting at the ancient holy city of Teotihuacan, the Tarzan company was attacked by Salvador Novo, Mexican playwright, director and critic, who wrote a blistering article declaring that the project had "degraded a national monument."

Under an agreement with the National Institute of Anthropology and History, a subsidiary of the Mexican Department of Education, Banner Productions was permitted to shoot for five days in the then recently excavated Aztec city and pyramids. The fee was 5,000 pesos ($400 U.S.) daily; plus an additional forty dollars daily for the presence of an Institute official to see that nothing was damaged. Weintraub also had to post a $40,000 bond to guarantee the premises would be left as found. And finally, the Teotihuacan villagers were paid $2,400 daily for their participation.

The contract for five days was honored, despite growing pressures on the Institute to get rid of the picture company. However, Weintraub's request for additional time was flatly refused; and a major sequence, at great cost, had to be staged at the Churubusco studios.

Mike Henry as a football star.

Before leaving Mexico, the official agency governing the production of all motion pictures in Mexico, asked that Weintraub surrender his 15,-000 feet of film for review. The producer was assured that the film was not being confiscated. They merely desired to learn whether the picture was derogatory to Mexico as Novo had charged. Containing nothing unfavorable, the film was returned.

At that point, Weintraub abandoned plans for further filming in Mexico and announced that Henry's next picture would probably originate in Madrid, and be called *Tarzan, Spain*.

While editing on *Tarzan and the Valley of Gold* progressed for an intended Christmas, 1965, release, arrangements were made to fly to Brazil to begin production on *Tarzan, Brazil*. Screenwriter Bob Barbash, scripting the details of an original story by Lewis Reed and himself, arbitrarily changed the title to *Tarzan and the Big River*, which after some deliberation became *Tarzan and the Great River*.

In late August, Mike and company were on their way to Rio de Janeiro for *Great River*, completion of which was to be followed by a short break. Then work was to begin on the TV series,

Mike Henry with Major, a seven-year-old lion, and Sharon Tate, who was originally intended for the part that went to Nancy Kovack.

178

The same shot with Nancy Kovack.

Mike Henry gives the ape-call.

which Weintraub had sold to NBC for the 1966-67 season.

Most of the animals used in the picture were flown in. The one that fascinated the Brazilians the most was the 500-pound trained lion, Major. The natives would crowd around him and, pointing, exclaim, "Leon!" In addition to being the number one attraction, the lion caused a few nerve-wracking incidents. "While shooting a scene in a downtown Rio public park," recalled Henry, "Major decided to take a stroll. He raced through the city streets with me on his tail. Before he chased after any of the scrambling pedestrians, I caught and returned him."

Things didn't always go that smoothly. In one scene, the lion, friendly to Tarzan, was to attack some unfriendly natives. Major took the attack to heart and bit one native on the foot. It made a realistic shot, albeit unusable.

"Those animals were unpredictable," swore Henry, from experience. "And it was dangerous working with them because none of the big cats we used had been de-toothed or de-clawed. Wild animals can never be tamed or trusted.

"For instance, in the second week of shooting," Mike continued, "we were working with

179

Henry and Nancy Kovack.

Tarzan attacked by a helicopter.

Nancy Kovack and Don Megowan in *Tarzan and the Valley of Gold*.

Don Megawan, David Opatashu, and Enrique Lucero.

Henry and Diana Millay in Paramount's *Tarzan and the Great River*, 1967.

181

Dinky the chimp, who seemed uneasy in his new environment. I was to run over to the chimp and pick him up. When I did, he lashed out at me and ripped my jaw open. It took twenty stitches to put my face back together. I was in a 'monkey-fever delirium' for three days and nights. It took me three weeks to recuperate."

While Mike was unable to work, director Bob Day had the script rewritten so they could shoot around him for awhile. The chimp had to be destroyed, and a different one appeared in the later scenes.

Co-starred with Mike in *Great River* was comedian Jan Murray, who played a river boat captain. Former Olympic decathlon champ Rafer Johnson supplied the villainy as Barcuna, the leader of a murderous leopard cult. And lovely Diana Millay was cast an an improbable jungle doctor, Ann Philips, who tried to innoculate the superstitious Brazilian Indians against an epidemic. The unwilling natives were convinced that there was nothing to fear in an immunization when Pepe (Manuel Padilla, Jr., again), Murray's young shipmate, took the first shot.

The picture was a unique experience for Jan Murray. In a key scene, he was supposed to fall into the river with a crocodile; Tarzan was then to rescue him. Jan balked.

"Go ahead. Jump in!" director Day called. "He's trained."

"Trained to do what?" Murray retorted.

"We don't know," Day humored him, "it's his first day here." The take went easily enough, but once Jan was out of the water, he quipped: "At

home I'm afraid of my miniature poodle. So here I am, acting with a lion, two monkeys, and a crocodile. I'm firing my agent, just as soon as I can get to a post office."

When *Great River* was finished, Mike was anxious to get home to rest before beginning the TV series, which was due to start in February. The intended break, however, was cancelled. It was decided to take advantage of the weather and squeeze in another feature before the heavy tropical storms hit. They had been on a seven-day-a-week work schedule fairly consistently. This meant that they would have to push a little harder. The strain became greater.

Mike Henry, who looks as though he could never be tired or overworked, began to feel the pressure. In addition to the illness from the monkey bite, he was plagued, like most of the others on the cast and crew, with food poisoning and dysentery. Then to make matters worse, during this next film, *Tarzan and the Jungle Boy*, he contracted an ear infection as the result of a fall. Doggedly, he continued shooting, only to be stricken with a virus infection of his liver.

After a quick trip home in early December while new sets were being constructed, Mike sped back to Brazil. There were deadlines that had to be met. A few weeks after his return, however, it began to rain heavily. The company heroically shot on, and literally had to fight the elements for each precious foot of film they got.

"It rained torturously for two weeks," recalled Mike. "The city's drainage system was unable to

182

handle the excessive rainfall. The Amazon River swelled and overflowed; and a typhoon struck, bringing the worst floods Rio had experienced in nearly a century. It'll take the city five years to recover.

"The floods broke the water mains, and all the running water in the buildings stopped. It took a week for the mains to be repaired. In the meantime to bathe, you had to order buckets of rain water from room service. It was the only thing available."

Many of the riverbank sets were destroyed and production ground to a halt. Another set on the beach was totally wiped out, incurring a loss of $140,000 for Weintraub. But the lost time was costing him much more.

Then, to add to the situation, a typhoid epidemic broke out. Playing the Good Samaritan, Sy had enough serum flown in to squelch it in a few days.

As soon as rains permitted, they were back at work, rebuilding washed-away sets and getting more of the *Jungle Boy* script on film. It dealt with a female reporter (Alicia Gure) and her fiancé (Ron Gans), who were conducting a search in the jungle for a wild boy (Steve Bond). Rafer Johnson stayed on to portray another heavy, and his real-life brother Eddie played his screen brother, who tried to set him straight. Where Eddie failed, Tarzan didn't.

The rains had put them far behind schedule. And because of the TV commitment, time was of

183

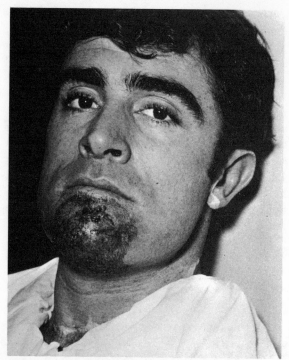

Mike Henry showing the bite of the chimpanzee.

the essence. They feverishly shot from dawn to dusk. Director Day informed the crew that there would be no break between the feature and the TV series now. They would have to continue the breakneck pace until they made up for the lost weeks.

Shortly before *Jungle Boy* was completely in the can, Mike, faced with remaining in Brazil indefinitely, told Weintraub that he was turning down the lead in the TV show. He was tired and his weakened health nagged him. He finished the picture and left for home. Weintraub told the press, "Mike's been in the jungle too long with those animals. It's enough to make a guy spooky. I would like him to continue in the feature Tarzans, but I will have to talk to him when he is less distraught."

The next Sy heard from Henry came in the form of two separate lawsuits against Banner Productions—one for $800,000 for "maltreatment, abuse, and working conditions detrimental to my health and welfare," and a second for $75,000, charging that the chimp bite "resulted from human error. Although the chimp chittered nervously just before that particular shot and I cautioned the director about it, he instructed me to do as I

184

Tarzan frightens Diana Millay.

Henry with Alicia Gure.

A karate chop.

was told and go ahead with the scene. And that's when I got bit."

Shortly after his return to civilization, Henry was offered the part of Batman in a feature movie, but because of the litigations with Banner Productions, he couldn't do it. The following months of bickering resolved nothing; it led only to hardened feelings. The suits still hang in abeyance.

Henry's next professional enterprise was a fiasco. He made a TV pilot for Screen Gems producer Harry Ackerman about a doltish hero called *Taygar, King of the Jungle,* whose mate (Kit Smythe) wore the family pants. Negro comedian George Kirby co-starred in the proposed satirical comedy.

Before the pilot found a sponsor, a $250,000 damage suit was filed by Banner Productions and Edgar Rice Burroughs, Inc., against Screen Gems, Inc., producer Ackerman, and Mike Henry. The suit asked for a court injunction forbidding production of the series, charging that *Taygar, King of the Jungle* was a deliberate attempt to burlesque and ridicule the Tarzan character." Henry insisted that it was not, and that the name Taygar was derived from Tiger, not Tarzan. But the dark clouds of a legal hangup prevented a sale, and the series was dropped.

After the Taygar series fell through, Henry went to work for Video Productions Incorporated, as a producer of TV commercials, and has been very successful.

Coinciding with his going to work for VPI in

June, 1966, was the release of *Tarzan and the Valley of Gold* by American International in Panavision and Eastmancolor. It is odd that Henry had finished three films as the Apeman and had vacated the role six months before his first Tarzan movie was shown anywhere. What a shame that Mike wasn't more dedicated to playing the jungle lord, because, even if his acting lacked motivation and confidence, he looked the part more than any of the Apemen, bar none. With a little experience and polish, he could have enhanced the series greatly.

Recognizing that it had been three years since the last Tarzan, Margaret Harford, *Los Angeles Times* staff writer, cheered: "It's fun to have the Apeman back even in a picture that offers nothing to ape over. . . . Henry makes a handsome, rather humorless Tarzan who looks just fine in a loincloth. Muscular as all get-out." *San Diego Union* critic James Meade's comment: "I am not sure how to review muscles." But *Photoplay* did: "This is a Tarzan that neither Johnny Weissmuller nor Buster Crabbe would recognize."

Fifteen months later, on September 12, 1967, Mike's second film, *Tarzan and the Great River,* was released by Paramount Studios. "It was inevitable," cried Tony Galluzo in the *Motion Picture Herald,* "that the classic jungle hero make the transition to modern times, even going so far as to sport the tailored Madison Avenue look." John Mahoney, in the *Hollywood Reporter,* appraised *Great River* as a "good action film . . . who cares that there are no hippos in the Ama-

186

Henry with Manuel Padilla, Jr., and Jan Murray.

Mike Henry and Steve Bond.

zon?" "In short," concluded Kevin Thomas for the *Los Angeles Times*, "this well-made movie, which has some beautiful scenery, is just right for the twelve-year-old mind, but is likely to bore anybody above this level."

Just prior to *Great River*'s release, Henry was signed for the role of the rugged Sgt. Kowalski in *The Green Berets*, a film by John Wayne's

Batjac Productions for Warner Brothers-Seven Arts. The film, which stars Wayne, David Janssen and Jim Hutton, was for three and a half months on location at Fort Benning, Georgia, for which Henry took a leave of absence from VPI.

Both *The Green Berets* and Henry's last Apeman film, *Tarzan and the Jungle Boy*, were released in the summer of 1968.

Ely wrestles with the lion that bit him on the forehead and thigh.

Ron Ely, the fifteenth Tarzan and first to appear on television, rides the elephant.

# 19 THE APEMAN SWINGS TO TELEVISION

On January 20, 1966, as Sy Weintraub jetted to Los Angeles from Brazil after learning that the disenchanted Henry was quitting, he burned with one question: "Who will replace Mike in the TV show?"

Forty-eight hours and a fast okay from NBC later, he was 'on his way back to Rio with Ron Ely, a six-foot-four, 210-pound Texas-born actor who bore a curious resemblance to his predecessor. The twenty-eight-year-old Ely had earlier been selected to portray Tarzan's impostor in a projected TV episode, and was merely shifted from pretender to the real thing. Ironically, he had been tested fourteen months earlier when Henry was given the part. Ely's past career comprised of a few inauspicious movie roles and co-star billing on TV's short-lived *Malibu Run*.

Upon arrival in Brazil, Ely was fitted with a thirty-dollar antelope loincloth, given a script and sent right to work, long before *Jungle Boy* concluded. Manuel Padilla, Jr., who had worked on

two pictures with Henry, stayed on to play Tarzan's ward for TV. Cheetah was to be third co-star.

Staying consistent with Weintraub's feature films, there was to be no Jane. "TV needs a sex symbol," said Sy, "and Ron has all the attributes. Provided he has no mate." Privately, Ron had had a mate, but was divorced.

At the location site, an hour and half from Rio, the frantic push began to do six hour-long episodes before the rainy season drove them out. It took an unprecedented five and a half months to do five shows. The torrential rains arrived early and within sixty days after the sets had been reconstructed following the history-making floods, they were washed away again. Roads leading to locations became impassable quagmires, trapping supply and production vehicles. Insects and reptiles were activated by the rain. Hoards of big, black barachuto mosquitoes bred in the standing puddles and were a constant nuisance in the

189

Ron Ely with Jill Donahue.

steambath humidity. The heat, dysentery and homesickness demoralized everyone. Tempers grew short and tensions were increased by communication difficulties with the natives.

Yet even with the overwhelming problems, they got some magnificent footage. The TV show's opening scenes were shot of Ron running along the 210-foot Iguazu Falls, located on the Argentinian-Brazilian border.' "Those falls make Niagara look like a faucet drip," exclaims Weintraub. "There's nothing else like it on the air. Viewers appreciate seeing it."

Ultimately, however, the weather won out. With the second producer, Jon Epstein, abandoning the post beside Weintraub, a $450,000 over-budget deficit, and only five episodes to show for it, the harried executive-producer ordered everything moved to Mexico.

The last scenes shot in Brazil brought relieved applause from everyone but Ely, who was required to sprint along the remaining streets of the $110,000 set, which had been set afire by associate producer, Steve Shagan, with the thought of using the footage in a later episode. Ron dodged the flames best he could, but his arms and legs were painfully singed. It was not his first injury, nor did he complain.

From the start, he had insisted on performing

190

Ely issues the ape-call.

his own stunts. From vine-swinging to fighting lions, he did it all, refusing the use of a double for anything. "I'm an actor," he said. "And I do what the part calls for. If I used a stunt man, I think I would be cheating the audience." At a much later date, he confessed, "I want to make the audience believe I *am* Tarzan." And he meant it.

In an early scene, he wrestled a tame lion, whose natural instinct was to get free. In the struggle he bit Ron on the forehead. "There was blood everywhere," Ely said. "At least it was realistic." Other pains suffered in Brazil by the fifteenth Apeman were a fall down a hill, ripping the skin off the tops of his feet, scratches from a puma and leopard.

Then in Mexico, a return bout with the same lion for an episode near Tepozotlan, about 150 miles south of Mexico City, resulted in Ron's being bitten on the left lower thigh.

Ely and Victoria Shaw.

James Whitmore with Ely.

From the television segment, "Hotel Hurricane."

With Sam Jaffe and Ulla Stromstedt.

191

Ely and Leta MacKenzie in the television segment, "Valley of the Unknown."

Ely battles a tiger.

192

During his first week in Mexico, he was doing a three-vine transfer in Chapultapec Park while hundreds of visitors looked on. He swung from the first vine, grabbed the second, but lost his grip and came short of the third. He fell twenty-five feet to the ground, landing on his left shoulder. He tried to get up, but fell back, unconscious. "To tell the truth," he said later, "I was embarrassed and wanted to show them I was all right."

The next morning, Ron's separated shoulder bones were wired back together in a two-hour operation. And after a week's rest, he was back on the set, adhesive tape protecting the surgical scar. The script had been rewritten to incorporate the fall, which had been recorded by two color cameras. A scene was inserted to show a villain shooting Tarzan down from the vine.

Then in another vine-swinging accident the rope broke and Ron again crashed to the ground, breaking his other shoulder, fracturing three ribs and spraining both wrists. Undaunted, Ely left the hospital within two weeks. For the next few episodes, Tarzan had his arm in a sling—a condition which was written into the script.

Before the Tarzan TV crew went on a break from the premiere season's shooting, Ron had suffered seventeen different injuries. "All *that* could've happened to the real Tarzan," grinned Ely, whose $3,000,000 insurance policy costs the producer $65,000 annually. Weintraub intends to increase it to five million and insist that Ron be replaced by a professional stuntman in dangerous scenes. "He just doesn't listen," moans Sy. "And he scares me. He actually believes that in a fight to the death with a 500-pound lion he could win."

Besides breaking all records for production injuries to previous Tarzans, Ron has created a more cultured, refined image of the Apeman. Although a bit too much like the boy next door, perhaps, and a little too collegiate, he is more like the hero that ERB dreamed up than any of his forerunners. He is not ornamented with huge muscles, but Burroughs created Tarzan with smooth, flowing, agile muscles, like Ron's. And his lines, somewhat prosey at times, are more natural than ever before: "Let's let out of here, this neighborhood's getting rough," "No time for fun and games," "There'll be room for every-

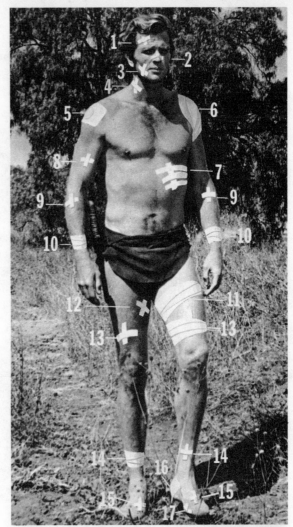

Ely's badges of combat from the first season of television shooting.

Ely with Mary Wilson and Diana Ross of The Supremes, in a Tarzan television episode, "The Convert."

Ely and Fernando Lamas in the television segment, "Jungle Ransom."

193

Ely with the most recent Cheetah.

In Mexico, Weintraub had made a deal with the Churubusco studios for twenty-five acres of dense jungle on the outskirts of the capital city. He spent nearly $200,000 in acquiring the land and constructing new sets approximating the old ones. The move in locations in late May, 1966, had brought in Leon Benson as Weintraub's producer.

Benson turned out five episodes in two months, but pulled out after tragedy struck. An elephant named Modak, thirty years old and weighing five tons, was used in the final episode that Benson produced. As Modak rested between scenes, a pack of stray dogs wandered on the set and angered the huge beast into a rampage. Modak

thing, except your self-pity," and "They're too smart to lose a decision to a puma."

"Ever read the original Tarzan stories?" Ron asked. "They're beautiful. About an educated man who returns to the environment he knows best, the jungle. There he seeks truth, honor, and man's lost humanity to man.

"This Tarzan is the part I've been waiting for all my life," he continued. "It's my big chance. I've never been in a quality series before. It's a good feeling. So good that I can't believe that I will ever be seriously hurt."

broke loose and headed in the direction of a woman and child. The trainer grabbed a stick and beat on the berserk animal to stop it. The enraged beast picked up the trainer and slammed him against a building, killing him, before it was shot to death.

Most of the crew were ready to call it quits on the seemingly jinxed show. What else could go wrong? But Benson persuaded everyone to get back to work. Then he himself quit. He was replaced by Steve Shagan who had been an associate since early Brazilian days.

By late August, 1966, a prematurely gray Weintraub had eleven episodes in the can. As total production for eight months, the pace was much too slow. But under the circumstances, he felt that his crews had performed a miracle.

195

Ely battles a tiger.

A Tarzan reunion in September, 1966. Jock Mahoney, Johnny Weissmuller, Ron Ely, and James H. Pierce.

Ely welcomes Weissmuller and Jim Pierce.

More of his hair turned gray when NBC informed Weintraub that *Tarzan's* premiere had been rescheduled from September 16 to September 8. The "sneak preview" on the Thursday preceding *Tarzan's* regular Friday night slot was in answer to ABC, which had at the last minute pushed its new shows ahead one week. Weintraub thought it would only confuse TV audiences as to what night his show was on, in addition to putting him another eight days behind.

In a scramble to get some national publicity in time for the September 8 airdate, NBC staged a reunion of former Tarzans at the Churubusco studios in Mexico. They had hoped to assemble ten ex-Apemen for a national magazine story. Only three showed up to pose with Ely: Johnny Weissmuller, James H. Pierce and Jock Mahoney, who was doing a *Tarzan* TV episode at the time, his hair crew-cut, and a heavy bruise discoloring his forehead. The photos of the four Tarzans together, spanning the years from the last silent feature in 1927 to the first TV series appeared in all the major papers across the country.

Regardless, Weintraub had been right about the sneak preview. In his review, Hal Humphrey, of the *Los Angeles Times*, wrote: "NBC sneaked *Tarzan* this Thursday (instead of Friday) to confuse the competition and the viewers." The episode that introduced the Apeman to TV featured Nara, a blind jungle princess, who got Tarzan to rescue her seeing-eye lion from natives that had mistaken it for a renegade that had killed one of their tribe.

Humphrey continued: "The ingredients seemed to be there for an exciting adventure, but it didn't play that way. The actors seemed bogged down in the dialogue, and badly paced direction made the hour much too long." Noted critic Cleveland Amory was of the same opinion: "We recommend *Tarzan* highly as a show to put the kids to bed by, but that's as far as we can go . . . A little boy named Jai (Manuel Padilla, Jr.) plays a part which is, if you can believe it, even sillier than Boy used to be in the old Tarzan films." Nevertheless, Johnny Weissmuller liked it: "I thought the show was good. But he's {Ely} a little on the thin side. . . ."

The early Nielsen ratings gave *Tarzan* a rocky start, ranking it fifty-first in a list of some 100 network shows, far below either of its competitors, *The Wild, Wild West* (CBS) and *The Green Hornet* (ABC). The show's poorest ratings were accrued on the five episodes filmed in Brazil. Weintraub admits these were not up to the standard they aimed for.

Once these five were aired and forgotten, the show improved; and by mid-December, *Tarzan* had climbed to twentieth place. The newer episodes filmed in Mexico were pepped up in quality to appeal to adult as well as kids. Ex-Tarzan Jock Mahoney showed up in a two-parter as a villain; and in a Brazil-filmed segment as a game warden.

The TV Tarzan's initial weakness had been converted to success by the end of the first season. "In my opinion," wrote Vern Coriell in *The Gridley Wave*, an amateur fan magazine, "The show improved considerably before the reruns started. Now if they would only come up with an episode that had Jai gobbled up by Gimla, the lizard."

It was only fitting that Hal Humphrey, who had criticized the show earlier, announced in March, 1967, that "*Tarzan* will be back again on TV next fall. Chiefly because NBC has found he had the largest audience of women between eighteen and thirty-four of any prime-time show, and also is second only to Lawrence Welk in cost-per-thousand viewers."

Then began the filming of the second season's segments. Still based in Mexico, *Tarzan* became branded by Hollywood trade unions as a "runaway production." "It's hard to convince everyone," producer Shagan, who had been in Mexico some fifteen months, finally spoke out, "that we can't get facilities in Hollywood. We couldn't afford the extensive layout that we have here.

"But shooting here like we do," he continued, "we encounter tremendous problems. You can just go so far working in an alien society, day in, day out, with no end in sight. It's a terribly depressing factor; loneliness and sickness greatly lowering the morale. The crews have no life except the show. I'm suffering from battle fatigue myself."

To break the routine of straight Mexican production, shows were planned elsewhere on location. A London segment was filmed in December, 1967; the story had Tarzan, Lord Greystoke, called back to England. A show was then shot in Guatemala, another in Mozambique.

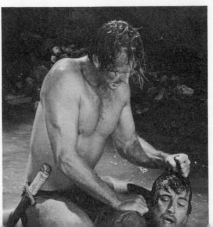

Ely and Gregg Palmer in the television segment, "Trek to Terror."

197

Julie Harris with Ely in a Tarzan television segment, "The Perils of Charity Jones."

Ely with Diahn Williams and Neville Brand.

Another policy initiated to improve quality as well as morale of the show, was the use of name guest stars. Ethel Merman, in a two-parter, led a group of hippies across the desert to establish a peace village. The Supremes, recording stars, played three nuns who sang their way across Africa to raise money for a mission. Other celebrities, so far, have included Julie Harris, Woody Strode, Helen Hayes and her son, James Mac-Arthur, Sam Jaffe, and Fernando Lamas. There is talk of using Johnny Weissmuller in a future episode.

Then, star Ron Ely turned director for a segment titled "Hurricane Hotel," filmed just days before the new TV season opened. Ely, who has received nothing but praise for the terrific job he's been doing as Tarzan, found himself in difficulties with the staff and crew, who resented his alleged high-handedness. Production chief Alfonzo Tello resigned and the crew threatened to walk out if "he doesn't get back up in the trees." Shagan quelled the tempest with the promise that Ely will not direct in the future. Tello returned a few hours later.

Sy Weintraub said that he investigated the affair and that it was "basically a language difference, a misunderstanding due to the inability to communicate wholly." He then added: "Ron did one of the best shows we've had . . . and will direct subsequent episodes in the series."

The September 15 premier show of *Tarzan* s second year on the NBC-TV network was called "Tiger, Tiger." Guest James Whitmore played an engineer who wanted to build an irrigation dam, but was opposed by natives who feared a rampaging tiger in the area. For this episode, Ely matched his brawn against a 350-lb. Bengal tiger, without being injured. "Jack Gillis wrote this segment," reported *Daily Variety*, "a vintage plot about a settler (Michael Pate) planting the big cat to terrify the natives, so they won't work on the irrigation project he opposes. The natives were restless, and so was the audience. . . . Maybe someone cut out some key scenes; it looked like it."

Although agreeing that the plotting and dialogue were uninspired, the weekly *Variety* stated that "*Tarzan* is one of the few strong shows on this otherwise tepid TV night." And James Powers, now editor of the *Hollywood Reporter*, analyzed that "the secret of success of *Tarzan* is the

198

willingness of the star to wrestle with the fauna while whipping through the flora. . . . The scenes of Ely taking on a large and energetic-looking tiger were done with a reality and versimilitude that may be unique in all man-animal pictures . . . Harmon Jones directed, and deserves credit— if for nothing elese—for persuading their star to undertake these strenuous and film-rewarding sequences."

A mid-season review of the Supremes' segment (aired on January 12, 1968) contained the following from Helm in the *Hollywood Reporter:* "Ely's topless and nearly bottomless covering exposes a physique that must have Ma peeking over the shrieking youngsters. Tarzan has gone through many tree-swingers over the years and . . . has lost none of his adventurous appeal. As long as there are new generations springing up, there'll be *Tarzan* and sponsors to pick up the tab."

The successful series was by now no longer owned by Sy Weintraub. On August 11, 1967, he had sold Banner Productions, and all affiliated companies, complete with twenty-eight old Tarzan features (which have all appeared on television), a large number of film properties and the TV *Tarzan* and related movie rights, to National General Corporation. They paid Sy $5,000,000 in National General Corporation convertible preferred stock and agreed to a later substantial additional consideration, contingent upon future earnings of the acquired companies. Later payment would be in non-convertible preference stock in the estimated amount of ten to fifteen million dollars.

According to his deal with NGC, Weintraub stayed on as executive vice-president of Banner in charge of production, TV and features.

A temporary threat to television production came on February 21, 1968, when NBC announced its new lineup for the 1968-1969 TV season. *Tarzan* was listed among the top shows which had been axed. But Weintraub was not overly concerned. "On a fairly consistent basis," he said, "*Tarzan* has had about a thirty percent share of the viewing audience, making it one of the highest rated shows ever to be dropped. I'm positive that we will have the show back on the air the following season, or possibly mid-season, on NBC

Ethel Merman in the television segment, " The Mountains of the Moon."

or another network. We will continue production to meet our present obligations, and then we'll prepare for the future, which also includes some feature films for Ron."

It is by no means the end of an era for Weintraub. His association with Tarzan of the Movies hardly seems to have begun. And if anyone deserved to make a fortune from the Tarzan character, other than ERB and his family, it is Sy Weintraub. He took the cliche-ridden, exhausted series from Sol Lesser and gave it style and elegance. The manner in which he made the Apeman a heavy grosser again parallels ERB's triumphant endeavor to make Tarzan into an industry.

Hulbert Burroughs, son of the great ERB and a vice-president of ERB, Inc., holds the most authoritative view of the situation. "I think Sy Weintraub has tried to make Tarzan more like the hero Dad created. Dad never liked the way Weissmuller played him—an inarticulate oaf. If you read Dad's book, you know that Tarzan was not like that."

Jimmy Durante as "Schnarzan", with Charles Butterworth
in MGM's *Hollywood Party*, 1934.

From the Russian film, *Tarzan Des Mers*, 1964.

APPENDIX

# WHAT ELSE?

Fifty years of Tarzan films could not have existed without a few satiric jabs at the Apeman by movie-makers. Oddly enough, Metro-Goldwyn-Mayer was the one to spoof ERB's hero, and at the time when he was most popular.

Shortly after the release of *Tarzan the Apeman*, producer Hal Roach, whose comedies were distributed by Metro, made a short called *Nature in the Wrong* (1932). Tarzan was portrayed by Charlie Chase, a skinny, bespectacled, Milquetoast comedian, who was the perfect antithesis of Weissmuller.

Two years later, while *Tarzan and his Mate* was packing them in, Jimmy Durante appeared as "Schnarzan" in MGM's *Hollywood Party*, a large-scale variety show which satirized the movie industry. Schnarzan's mate was Phyllis Crane, who portrayed Jane clad in an oversized fig leaf.

Spoofs on Tarzan using his actual name have been limited because of the strict control exercised over the film rights to the character. How-

ever, protecting these rights in the realm of unauthorized adventure films has been as difficult as it has been in the field of book and magazine publishing.

The earliest known unauthorized Tarzan movie was *The Adventures of Chinese Tarzan*. Produced by the Hsin Hwa Motion Picture Company of Singapore in 1940, it was to have been the first of a series. The Apeman was incredibly portrayed by one Peng Fei, and Lee Cha Cha appeared as Jane Porter. Although the picture played to long lines in Shanghai, no sequals materialized.

Alongside unauthorized productions were pirated films. While in New York on business in 1944, Sol Lesser was called by a Turkish film distributor who told him that he had a Turkish Tarzan film for sale. Intrigued by the idea, Lesser set up a screening of the film, after which he confiscated it legally. This film was one of Lesser's own productions, *Tarzan's Revenge* (1938),

Lee Chacha and Peng Fei in *The Adventures of Chinese Tarzan*, 1939.

with Glenn Morris. The Turks had dubbed it and ingeniously cut in the face of a Turkish actor whenever a closeup of Morris appeared.

Ralph Rotmund, long-time general manager of ERB, Inc., in 1954 stopped production of a series of Tarzan films in India after three had been made. Apparently, the Berar Region-based operation had ground out quick films for distribution in Nigeria.

In 1963, unauthorized activity increased horrendously, due to the erroneous idea that certain Tarzan properties were in the public domain. Sy Weintraub and ERB, Inc., impressed claim-jumpers with the fact that they should have checked into the matter before going ahead with costly production.

Cosmopolis Films, a French distributor now reportedly in bankruptcy, was prevented by ERB, Inc., and Banner Productions from handling an Italian-made Tarzan film called *Tarzan, Roi de la*

*Force Brutale.* The film, which was made by Italia Produzione and Coronet Produzioni, starred Joe Robinson as the Apeman. It was seized and released only when the producers agreed to change the lead character's name to *Thaur* before showing it anywhere.

In another suit, Weintraub's laywers confiscated the negative to *Tarzan chez les Coupers de Têtes,* a French film made by an Italian company.

While in Paris for the above case, counsel for Burroughs and Banner also kept Liberal Films from distributing a Russian-made picture called *Tarzan des Mers,* which dealt with an amphibious man, Iktiandre (Vladimir Korenev), who was washed up on the beach. The film was eventually exhibited under the title of *The Amphibious Man.*

A fourth picture, *Tarzan and the Jewels of Opar,* was stopped after three days of production in Jamaica. Robert Hodes, then legal counsel and

Joe Robinson in the unauthorized Italian film, *Tarzan, Roi de la Force Brutale.*

Don Bragg, the 1960 Olympic champion who played the lead in the unauthorized *Tarzan and the Jewels Of Opar.*

## 'TARZAN AND CIRCUS'

OPENING next week at the Rex Cinema, Onitsha is a Sargaam Chittra release, "TARZAN AND CIRCUS", starring Chitra, Azad, Sheri, Rajan Kapoor and Sunder with Lou Anderegg and Christine Keeler as co-stars.

"Tarzan and Circus," is a story of a charming young man who is brought up in the company of wild animals and who has forgotten everything... even himself.

Ring master of the circus, who has lost all the happiness of his life with the loss

of his only son is Nandan. He loved his son more than even his own life.

Bimla, the proprietress of the circus who has everything at her disposal... everything except LOVE for which she has been craving always... but without luck.

Malti, the pupil of Nandam... she aspires to become the ring master one day and bestowes her soul and heart on the young and charming Tarzan.

The wicked manager of the circus whose every attempt is to capture the wealth of Bimla and the youth of Malti.

What plans they made, what hardships they underwent and what sufferings they came across to achieve their respective goals can be known when you see the film, "Tarzan and Circus" in the next few days at the Rex Cinema, Onitsha.

— CRITIC

Clipping from a Nigerian newspaper.

now general manager of ERB, Inc., won an injunction against Jamaica Pictures Ltd., headed by Sherman S. Krellberg and Sandy Howard, and filming was permanently suspended on November 18, 1964. The suit that followed, in which the verdict was delivered to the plaintiff, was the first copyright case ever to be tried in Jamaica, and as such set precedents.

Featured as Tarzan in this film was Don Bragg, 1960 Olympic champion pole-vaulter, whose life's ambition had been to portray the Apeman on the screen. The six-foot-two, 200-pounder grumbled that producers "always use a body-builder—some guy who has muscles for show, not for athletics. You can't conceive of guys like that doing the things Tarzan has to do." The entire crew had been brought to the location from New York.

Things were not over by any means. A quick trip to Czechoslovakia prevented distribution of a movie called *The Death of Tarzan*. And when a new U.S. company headed by director Ray Dennis and scripter Ron Haydock announced plans to shoot *Jungle Tales of Tarzan* in Thousand Oaks, California, Hodes informed them of ERB, Inc.'s legal position. Although the cast was all set, with Brick Bardo and Carolyn Brandt headlining, the picture was not heard of again.

Hodes then learned that Sargaam Chittra, Ltd., an Indian movie company, had cranked out ten Tarzan films between 1963 and 1965. An Indian wrestler named Darasingh played the Jungle Lord in the first four: *Rocket Tarzan, Tarzan and Delilah, Tarzan and King Kong* and *Tarzan Comes*

207

to *Delhi*. The role then went to a younger fellow called Azad, who completed six films co-starred with "the beautiful Chitra as his mate." Their pictures were: *Tarzan and Cleopatra, Tarzan and the Gorilla, Tarzan's Beloved, Tarzan and Magician, Tarzan and Captain Kishore,* and *Tarzan and Circus.* Released in August, 1965, *Circus* featured Christine Keeler as ,the proprietress of the traveling show and carnival.

As with the Indian films made in the early fifties, these "quickie" productions were exclusively for distribution in Nigeria. And as before, further activity was stopped and existing negatives seized.

The front is quiet now. And Edgar Rice Burroughs, Inc., hopes that it will remain that way. However, Bob Hodes stands ready to catch the first available jet to any location in the world where it is even rumored that an unauthorized Tarzan film may be in the works.

Charlie Chase as Tarzan in the MGM Hal Roach comedy, *Nature in the Wrong,* 1932.

The Tarzan family à la Hal Roach.